Hebrews

INTERPRETATION
BIBLE STUDIES

Hebrews

EARL S. JOHNSON, JR.

Westminster John Knox Press
LOUISVILLE • LONDON

Scripture quotations from the New Revised Standard Version of the Bible are copyright © 1989 by the Division of Christian Education of the National Council of the Churches of Christ in the U.S.A. and are used by permission.

Excerpt from Earl S. Johnson, Jr., "The Universe Is God's," *Presbyterian Outlook*, August 28, 2006, is reprinted by permission of the *Presbyterian Outlook*. All rights reserved.

Excerpt from Earl S. Johnson, Jr., "A Pioneer Faith," *Presbyterian Outlook* June 4, 2006, is reprinted by permission of the *Presbyterian Outlook*. All rights reserved.

The diagram on p. 15 is © John Knox Press, 1997. All rights reserved. Used by permission. The photographs on p. 25, *Moses Breaking the Tablets of the Law, Exodus* by Gustave Dore (1832–83) (after), Private Collection/ Ken Welsh/ The Bridgeman Art Library; p. 39, *Tabernacle and Court in the Wilderness (Solomon's Temple)*, 19th century, litho, Private Collection/ The Bridgeman Art Library; p. 44, *The Erection of the Tabernacle by the Children of Israel in the Wilderness* (engraving) (b&w photo) by English School (19th century), Private Collection/ The Bridgeman Art Library; p. 45, Peter Paul Rubens, Flemish, 1577–1640, *The Sacrifice of the Old Covenant* (detail), about 1626, Oil on panel, 70.5 × 87.6 cm (27 3/4 × 34 1/2 in.), Museum of Fine Arts, Boston, Gift of William A. Coolidge, 1985.839, © 2007 Museum of Fine Arts, Boston. All rights reserved; p. 65, *Christian sarcophagus* (marble) by Roman (3rd century AD) Santa Maria Antiqua, Rome, Italy/ Alinari/ The Bridgeman Art Library are used with permission. All rights reserved.

Book design by Drew Stevens
Cover design by Pam Poll
Cover illustration by Robert Stratton

First edition
Published by Westminster John Knox Press
Louisville, Kentucky

This book is printed on acid-free paper that meets the American National Standards Institute Z39.48 standard. ♾

PRINTED IN THE UNITED STATES OF AMERICA

08 09 10 11 12 13 14 15 16 17 — 10 9 8 7 6 5 4 3 2 1

Library of Congress Cataloging-in-Publication Data

Johnson, Earl S.
    Hebrews / Earl S. Johnson, Jr. — 1st ed.
        p. cm. — (Interpretation Bible studies)
    ISBN 978-0-664-23190-3 (alk. paper)
    1. Bible. N.T. Hebrews—Commentaries.   I. Title.
    BS2775.53.J63 2008
    227'.8707—dc22   2007045710

Let us run with perseverance the race that is set before us,
looking to Jesus the pioneer and perfecter of our faith.
(Hebrews 12:1b–2)

Contents

Series Introduction

The Bible has long been revered for its witness to God's presence and redeeming activity in the world; its message of creation and judgment, love and forgiveness, grace and hope; its memorable characters and stories; its challenges to human life; and its power to shape faith. For generations people have found in the Bible inspiration and instruction, and, for nearly as long, commentators and scholars have assisted students of the Bible. This series, Interpretation Bible Studies (IBS), continues that great heritage of scholarship with a fresh approach to biblical study.

Designed for ease and flexibility of use for either personal or group study, IBS helps readers not only to learn about the history and theology of the Bible, understand the sometimes difficult language of biblical passages, and marvel at the biblical accounts of God's activity in human life, but also to accept the challenge of the Bible's call to discipleship. IBS offers sound guidance for deepening one's knowledge of the Bible and for faithful Christian living in today's world.

IBS was developed out of three primary convictions. First, the Bible is the church's scripture and stands in a unique place of authority in Christian understanding. Second, good scholarship helps readers understand the truths of the Bible and sharpens their perception of God speaking through the Bible. Third, deep knowledge of the Bible bears fruit in one's ethical and spiritual life.

Each IBS volume has ten brief units of key passages from a book of the Bible. By moving through these units, readers capture the sweep of the whole biblical book. Each unit includes study helps, such as maps, photos, definitions of key terms, questions for reflection, and suggestions for resources for further study. In the back of each volume is a Leader's Guide that offers helpful suggestions on how to use IBS.

The Interpretation Bible Studies series grows out of the well-known Interpretation commentaries (Westminster John Knox Press), a series that helps preachers and teachers in their preparation. Although each IBS volume bears a deep kinship to its companion Interpretation commentary, IBS can stand alone. The reader need not be familiar with the Interpretation commentary to benefit from IBS. However, those who want to discover even more about the Bible will benefit by consulting Interpretation commentaries too.

Through the kind of encounter with the Bible encouraged by the Interpretation Bible Studies, the church will continue to discover God speaking afresh in the scriptures.

Introduction to Hebrews

Why Read Hebrews?

It is not often, in most churches, that classes or sermons are offered on the Letter to the Hebrews. For most modern Christians the book is too difficult to understand, so obscure, so steeped in Old Testament imagery and complicated arguments about ancient sacrificial systems that it is bypassed in favor of other books. Attention is further deflected by its structure. Readers wonder why it is so repetitive and so complicated in its form of argument.

Yet the message of Hebrews keeps calling to twenty-first-century readers, and we ignore it at our peril. The key focus on Jesus Christ and his superiority to all heavenly beings and human leaders, its emphasis on faith in what cannot be seen, its insistence that covenants and contracts really matter (especially those with God and other believers) are all critical issues of faith today. They provide direction for those who feel lost in a world that appears enamored with relative values and is constantly worried about issues of ultimate survival.

The original recipients of Hebrews faced situations like our own. They lived in a violent world dominated by Jewish terrorist groups on one hand and by the power of a brutal Roman military machine on the other. Their faith was shaky, they feared the worst, and they wondered if God could still save them. The old forms of belief no longer gave them comfort and structure, and they needed to move beyond familiar stories of spiritual heroes and the concept that redemption came mainly through the ritual of animal sacrifice to a new message that bridged the gap between Old Testament concepts of faith and new hope in the future through Jesus Christ.

If we are understandably anxious today about the possible irreversible danger of global warming, the destruction that could be caused by worldwide bioterror and nuclear attacks, and the constant pressures of being peacemakers in a violent world, there is much to learn from Hebrews. The first readers were also faced with the possibility of the ending of their world as they knew it since Rome had already destroyed (or was poised to destroy) a nation that was trying to defy its power. They needed a guide and a force to lead them to faith (12:2). Their drooping hands and weak knees had to be strengthened (12:12). They desperately longed for a word of encouragement and exhortation (13:22) to give them endurance, confidence, and hope (12:7–13; 13:5–6).

Hebrews draws readers, modern or ancient, back to the centrality of faith in Jesus Christ and the certain knowledge that God will keep all believers in powerful love, no matter when, no matter what. The author reassures them not only with a message to the heart but also with intellectual arguments that are still persuasive today, once their purpose and structure are understood.

New Understandings

Although it seems easy to get lost in the complex line of reasoning and digressions that Hebrews presents, recent studies of its purpose and background demonstrate that the book is very carefully and precisely written and reflects the work of a creative literary craftsman. The style of writing used in Hebrews is called *rhetoric* and was very familiar to readers of Greek literature in the first century CE. Examinations of the text by textual linguistics and discourse analysis show that the letter was written to be read aloud (probably as a long sermon or oral argument) and that the use of repetition, catchwords, digressions, the frequent reuse of the same Old Testament passages, and chain-link transitions that close and open one section with the same words and concepts were considered devices that a good writer used to make the sermon easier to listen to and remember. What is more, new research into the political and sociological background of the letter, the ideas of honor and shame in the ancient world (saving face), for example, make it possible to see this book through the eyes of its first readers. These insights bring today's Bible students closer to its original meaning and enable them to connect it to their own lives.

Studying the homily of Hebrews (or should we call it a spiritual lecture?) can be very exciting. It is like going down a road you have traveled before, one where all the landmarks are familiar, only to discover this time that there are billboards, people, houses, streams, and side roads that you never noticed before. And suddenly the trip is no longer routine but becomes an adventure as you explore a whole new world.

The Purpose of This Study

Hebrews is a difficult book to understand. Those who work in the original Greek know how hard it is to translate, how complex some of its arguments are. The vocabulary used is often found only here or in one or two other New Testament books. Because the amount of research published on this book is voluminous, moreover, it is impossible to cover all the important issues of interpretation that this important book raises. Instead, focus is concentrated here on the needs of those who are likely to be reading this book: pastors looking for biblical themes of importance for sermons, teachers preparing to explain Hebrews' mysteries to adult and young adult students, groups gathering in the church lounge or someone's living room to seek a fresh word from the Lord, and individuals hoping to deepen their faith and rebuild their spiritual confidence. It can only be hoped that all these searchers will find what is written here stimulating and encouraging as they move along on their own Christian journeys.

Ten Key Passages in Hebrews

1:1–2 "Long ago God spoke to our ancestors . . . , but in these last days . . . by a Son."

2:1 "We must pay greater attention to what we have heard."

3:1–2 "Jesus, the apostle and high priest of our confession, was faithful to the one who appointed him."

4:12 "The word of God is living and active, sharper than any two-edged sword."

6:1 "Let us go on toward perfection."

8:6–7 "Jesus has now obtained a more excellent ministry, and to that degree he is the mediator of a better covenant, which had been enacted through better promises. For if that first covenant had been faultless, there would have been no need to look for a second one."

10:24 "Let us consider how to provoke one another to love."

11:1 "Faith is the assurance of things hoped for, the conviction of things not seen."

12:1 "We are surrounded by . . . a cloud of witnesses."

13:8 "Jesus Christ is the same yesterday and today and forever."

What Kind of Book Is It?

Although it is often referred to as an epistle, Hebrews is not really a letter in a standard sense. Unlike the letters of Paul, it is not addressed to individual readers and it does not deal with problems of a particular church community. Instead, it is more like a long generic sermon or stump speech, perhaps a theological instructional lecture that is concerned with the dangerous and perplexing circumstances that many congregations were facing. The author simply calls it "my word of exhortation" (13:22), that is, a message of comfort and encouragement, a spiritual motivational speech. Since it deals so much with Old Testament images and issues around the Jerusalem Temple and the value of the priesthood, it was probably written for Jewish Christians. If we look at all the Old Testament references in Paul's letters, however, most of which were written for Gentiles, it is not difficult to imagine that Hebrews spoke powerfully to non-Jewish converts as well. We do not know where the people lived who read it or what their exact circumstances were.

Want to Know More?

About Hebrews See Frances Taylor Gench, *Hebrews and James,* Westminster Bible Companion (Louisville, Ky.: Westminster John Knox, 1996); Daniel J. Harrington, *What Are They Saying about the Letter to the Hebrews?* (Mahway, N.J.: Paulist Press, 2005); Luke Timothy Johnson, *Hebrews: A Commentary,* New Testament Library (Louisville, Ky.: Westminster John Knox Press, 2006); Thomas G. Long, *Hebrews: A Bible Commentary for Teaching and Preaching* (Louisville, Ky.: Westminster John Knox Press, 1997).

Who Was the Author?

The view that was once widely held—that Paul may have written Hebrews—has largely been discarded in the last hundred years. It is has little similarity to his other writings and it appears to reflect circumstances quite different from the ones that usually concerned him. Theories that Paul's companions Barnabas or Apollos, or his financial supporter Priscilla, composed it are provocative but equally difficult to prove. The precise identity of the writer and his or her background are unknown to us, and if it was ever evident to the original readers, the information must have been lost as the sermon was copied and passed along from church to church. Whoever it was, the writer was obviously someone who was highly literate and was a Christian of deep faith who had a vision of hope to share during tough times.

When Was It Written?

Arguments have been made for a variety of possible dates when the sermon in Hebrews was written, some early in the Christian era and some toward the end of the first century. Although it is impossible to pin down the date with any certainty, most scholars think that it is likely that it was composed at a time just before or at a time after the Roman destruction of Jerusalem and the Temple of Herod in 70 CE. The preoccupation with the lack of spiritual value in animal sacrifice, the denigration of the worship offered at one time in the Temple, and Jesus' superiority over the Jewish high priest might indicate, on the other hand, that the attack had already happened some time ago but was still fresh in the minds of the readers. An analysis of 10:32–39 and the comparison of the situation described there with those found in late first-century Christian writings like 1 and 2 Peter and Jude point to the strong possibility that Hebrews may be one of the last books of the New Testament to have been written (see the discussion in Unit 8, pp. 51–52).

1

Jesus Christ Is the Exact Representation and Reflection of God's Radiance

Present in the Rhythm of God's Creation

The book of Hebrews begins with the highest and most lofty view of Jesus Christ imaginable. Rather than starting the sermon with Jesus' family tree and birth as the Gospels of Matthew and Luke do, or with his baptism (Mark), the author looks to the farthest regions of the universe to discover the origins of Jesus' radiance and splendor.

To put it in modern terms, it is as if the Hubble Space Telescope were to be focused far beyond the brilliance of the nearby Milky Way to look at the primal light coming from the very edge of the universe. According to Hebrews, Jesus was present at the time of the big bang and the creation of what astronomers now call "the first light." He participated in the rhythm and energy of God's creation. The light we see in him, however, is not just the radiation from billions of years ago but the present brilliance of God's presence and the hope that will enlighten the world in the future through the Son.

This argument from absolute superiority is maintained throughout the sermon, as our outline clearly shows. Before time even began, he was "the exact imprint of God's very being." He is greater than all heavenly beings (angels), superior to the prophets and messengers from the past, and more powerful than all religious and political leaders. He alone provides a new covenant in alliance with God, a renewed hope, a better promise, and a faith in things that are so brilliant they cannot be seen. There is nothing, no one, no doctrine, no military force, that can outshine him.

How God Speaks to Us Now

The author of Hebrews demonstrates his poetic talent and literary training in the very first verse with an alliterative introduction in which *five* Greek words beginning with P outline the new age in Christ : " Long ago (*palai*), God spoke to our ancestors (*patrasin*) in many (*polymerōs*) and various ways (*polutropōs*) by the prophets (*prophētais*), but in these last days he has spoken to us by a Son." They indicate that although human beings have received God's Word from the prophets in the past, in this present time of expectation and danger ("these last days"), the message now comes from a Son who is greater than anyone who has gone before him. He was the Son from the beginning, but through his suffering, death, and resurrection ("*made purification for sins*"), he has been raised to an even higher rank (if this can be imagined), on "*the right hand*" (the choice place of power) of God.

> **Other Biblical Texts about the Superiority of Christ**
>
> 1 Corinthians 8:6 "One Lord, Jesus Christ, through whom are all things and through whom we exist."
>
> Colossians 1:15 "He is the image of the invisible God, the firstborn of all creation."
>
> John 1:1–2 "In the beginning was the Word, and the Word was with God, and the Word was God."
>
> Revelation 22:13 "I am the Alpha and the Omega, the first and the last, the beginning and the end."

The language and arguments here probably come from a threefold blend of ideas taken from Greek philosophy, the interpretation of Hebrew scriptures, and the author's own unique understanding of the Christian faith. In the writings of Plato, for example, it is stated that reality is not found so much in what is observed directly, but in shadow and reflection, in what is not seen (Heb. 11:1, for example). In various discussions of the coming of the Messiah in the Hebrew prophets, furthermore, it is shown how the plan of God will be revealed in a new age. In the first verses of Hebrews, the author shows how both of these concepts become a reality for Christian believers in the presence of Jesus, who reflects the truth ancient people searched for, the one predicted long ago in the scriptures.

Key Terms That Show Who Jesus Really Is

In verses 3–5 some unusual vocabulary is used that helps pull the three concepts together. Two key Greek words are used only here in the New Testament: "reflection" (*apaugasma*) and "exact imprint" (*charaktēr*). Three others are found in Hebrews and only one other New Testament book: "very being" (*hypostasis*, see 2 Cor. 9:4; 11:17), "majesty" (*megalōsunē*, Jude 25), and "more excellent"(*diaphoros*, Rom. 12:6). All five words are piled up to give an overwhelming impression of the brilliance, power, and prominence of Jesus and show how unique he is. Although they are occasionally used in ancient literature to describe other gods and heavenly beings, the author of Hebrews wants to convince readers that Jesus is the only one who really deserves them.

Since these words are carefully chosen at the beginning of the sermon, it is important to learn a little more about what they mean. *Reflection*, for example, refers to the light that comes from another source, like that from the moon. It can also describe the actual radiance of the object itself—what is seen by gazing directly into the sun. By looking at Jesus, Hebrews says, we see the very light of God. This same word is used in the Apocrypha to describe God's wisdom: "For she is a reflection of eternal light, a spotless mirror of the working of God, and an image of his goodness" (Wis. 7:26). *Exact imprint* means that what is seen is not a mere copy of God or a picture, but the precise likeness. It is the most faithful representation possible, a trademark, a stamp, like the face of a king or emperor on a coin. The word translated *very being* makes the impact even stronger. It points to the essence or heart of something, its true nature or core. In the fourth century, it was used by the church in the Nicene Creed to teach that Jesus is not just like God, but truly is God, "God of God, Light of Light, Very God of Very God, begotten not made. . . ." Jesus is the *majesty* of God itself (Heb. 8:1), or as Jude 25 puts it, he

Key Terms

Exact Imprint   The mark on an object, a stamp, engraving, or trademark; a reproduction or representation

Glory   The weight or worth of God. " The term 'glory'. . . is used in Scripture with reference above all to the visible presence of God among the people." (Luke Timothy Johnson, 69)

Majesty   The unique power, sovereignty, and dignity of God as ruler or king

Reflection   The reflection of a bright object or its direct radiance or brightness

Very Being   The essential or basic structure of a thing or person; the reality, actual quality

is the "glory, majesty, power, and authority, before all time and now and forever." His name is more excellent than that of the angels, and he provides *a more excellent ministry* (Heb. 8:6). As Paul writes in Philippians 2:9–10, God "highly exalted him and gave him the name that is above every name, so that at the name of Jesus every knee should bend, in heaven and on earth and under the earth."

Jesus' superlatives are summed up in Hebrews 1:4 where it is said that he is *superior*, a Greek word (*kreittōn*) used repeatedly in the sermon to indicate how great he is. Better things come through him (6:9; 10:34). He provides a better hope (7:19), a more advantageous covenant (8:6; 12:24), more effective sacrifices (9:23), a higher destiny (11:16), and a "better resurrection" (11:35, 40).

The Universe Is God's

To the Tune "Now Thank We All Our God"
6.7.6.7.6.6.6.6

The universe is God's, Who framed the whole Creation,
All praises be to God, Who made the constellations.
The distant space reveals, An outline and intent,
Faint blueprint of a plan, Its wonder and extent.

Our Voyagers explore, The planets' farthest reaches,
We survey spiral arms, Through interstellar searches.
We look for your first light, And probe the ancient stars,
Our telescopes are poised To find out who we are.
Earl S. Johnson, Jr.
Outlook, August 28, 2006, Printed by Permission

Getting Ready for the Next Section in Verse 4

The introduction in 1:1–4 ends in a way that is characteristic of the author's style of writing, and we will see it over and over again. Often called a "chain link" transition, it connects one part of the sermon to what comes next by the repetition of concepts and words. In verses 3 and 4, the idea that Jesus sits on the *right hand* of God and is *superior* to the *angels* sets the stage for what follows in 1:5–14, where several Old Testament scriptures demonstrate what all three of these ideas mean: angels (1:5, 6, 7), right hand (1:13), and Jesus' eternity (1:10,12) and superiority (1:14)

? Questions for Reflection

1. Hebrews 1:1–4 is like the Doxology that many Christians sing in worship every Sunday, a description of God's glory in Christ. Read the similar piling up of words of praise in Romans 11:33–36. What are believers trying to do when they describe the wonder and power of the living God in such a way?

2. Scientists often refer to the radiation created by the "big bang" as the "first light." Read Hebrews 1:1–4 and compare these verses to Genesis 1:1–5 and John 1:1–9. What connection can you see between light as a building block of the universe and the light of Christ?

3. Do think that Christ was actually present with God at the time of creation, or is this merely symbolic language used to describe his greatness?

4. Does the repetition of ideas and words help you understand Hebrews better? Take a look at Ecclesiastes 3 and see how a similar style of writing is used there to make the text memorable.

2 Hebrews 1:5–14

Jesus Christ Is Greater than All God's Messengers and Servants

The Old Testament Witnesses to Christ

Imagine that one Sunday in the service of worship a member of the church introduces a new hymn she has just written which expresses the greatness of Jesus. Even though you might not know where all the words come from, perhaps from the Old Testament ("There is no Holy One like the LORD"), or the New Testament ("the beginning and the end"), or a popular hymn ("How Great Thou Art"), you could still join in and be moved by the experience because you do know who Christ is. The same would be true if the hymn is illustrated by pictures of Christ projected on a screen. If you do not know whether an artwork is by Michelangelo, Rembrandt, or El Greco, you still understand what is meant because Christ is known to you.

The book of Hebrews introduces the first references to the greatness of Christ by assembling a number of images and texts from the Old Testament that are put together to honor him. It is possible that they were originally collected in the early church for use as a liturgy, a confession of faith, or even as a hymn. Similar passages in the New Testament began as hymns, and they also stress Jesus' equality with God and his superiority over all angels and human leaders (see Phil. 2:6–11; Col. 1:15–18; Eph. 1:20–23; 1 Pet. 3:22).

In Hebrews 1:5–14 the author collects snippets of seven different Old Testament texts that are listed one after another to show that Jesus Christ is the one mentioned in them. Although it may be diffi-

---

Seven Old Testament Texts

Psalm 2:7
Deuteronomy 32:43
Psalm 104:4
Psalm 45:6–7
Isaiah 61:1, 3
Psalm 102:25
Psalm 110:1

---

cult for twenty-first-century Christians to identify which books these passages come from, they were probably well known to the original listeners who had heard them put together before. A similar collection is found in the introduction to Mark's Gospel. Even though he refers to them as coming from Isaiah, the first one is actually from Malachi. A similar chorus of texts is found in Romans 11:33–36, where Paul praises the glory of God.

For modern Christians the listing of Old Testament texts to prove that Jesus is God's Son might not be entirely convincing. But the first readers had such a respect for the Hebrew Bible that they believed that if you could show how God prepared the way for the Son, even before he was born, you had demonstrated the authenticity of his divinity and power.

The author of the book of Hebrews uses texts in other ways, furthermore, that are not familiar to us. The version of the Old Testament that is quoted is not from the original Hebrew but from the translation in Greek known as the Septuagint. In some places the Greek differs considerably and seems to make the point stronger (compare the text in 1:7 to Psalm 104:4 in the NRSV). The author also manipulates the significance of the passage on occasion to make the connection with Christ more obvious.

Early Christians were able to use the Old Testament in such ways because they were not worried about plagiarism or being accused of falsifying evidence. For the readers of Hebrews, the words did more than provide information about

> Reading Heb 1 is something like looking at a mosaic that depicts the image of a person. . . . Those who look at the mosaic generally do not ask where the individual pieces came from or how each piece functioned elsewhere, but whether the arrangement of the stones conveys a genuine likeness of the person being portrayed. Similarly, to read Heb 1 on the author's own terms is to ask whether the mosaic of OT quotations is a faithful presentation of the exalted Christ. (Koester, 198)

their original meaning. Through them God spoke directly in the present time about Jesus. As it is put in 4:12, the Word of God is not a dead letter, but is living and active. When Psalm 2:7 is quoted in Hebrews 1:5, for example, it is not speaking to the king (the original context) but to Jesus himself. In verse 8 the reference is not to the inauguration of the royal sovereign (original context) but the raising up of Jesus to power. In other places the author points out how God speaks to the readers in the present tense (4:3; 5:5, 6; 12:5–6). Occasionally, it is imagined that Jesus is so present with God from the beginning that the words in the Hebrew Bible are coming from his mouth (2:3, 12, 13; 10:5, 7) or from the Holy Spirit (3:7; 10:15, 17).

Even though modern Christians might not present evidence about Christ's greatness in the same way, it is important to appreciate the significance of the message that the opening hymn is trying to convey.

—No angel was ever called God's Son.
—The angels must worship the Son, who is of higher status.
—The power of God is one with the power of the Son.
—Although the heavens and the earth will perish, the might of God is forever.
—Jesus sits at God's right hand, at the place of highest honor and privilege.

Why Angels?

Why does the author go to such great lengths to distinguish Jesus from angels and insist on his prominence over them? In the Bible angels are messengers who speak in God's name. They are heavenly beings who can call people to service (see Luke 1:26–27; Acts 10:3), punish offenders (Rev. 9:14–15), deliver messages of great joy (Matt. 1:18–25; Luke 1:11, 13, 26–38; 2:9–10), witness to the resurrection (Matt. 28:1–10; Mark 16:1–8; Luke 24:4–5), and even bring a sermon to churches (Rev., chaps. 2; 3).

Possibly the listeners to Hebrews were worshiping angels and attributing more power to them than they were to Christ. Perhaps they were trying to distinguish between evil and good angels and wanted to know how Jesus related to them. Maybe they were confused by the fact that even though Jesus was the Son of God from the beginning, he became a human being who was lower than the angels for a time (Heb. 2:5–8). Whatever concept they struggled with, it is made clear that *now,* after his suffering, death, and resurrection, Jesus outranks all heavenly beings and has control over them all. As Paul says in Romans 8:38–39, "I am convinced that neither death, nor life, nor angels, nor rulers, nor things present, nor things to come, nor powers, nor height, nor depth, nor anything else in all creation, will be able to separate us from the love of God in Christ Jesus our Lord."

Want to Know More?

About Angels? See Susan R. Garrett, *No Ordinary Angel* (New York: Doubleday, 2007); Maxwell John Davidson, "Angel," in *The New Interpreters' Dictionary of the Bible*, vol. 1, A–C (Nashville: Abingdon Press, 2006).

One way to illustrate what is happening is with the "Parabola of Salvation" developed by Thomas Long.

Although Jesus Christ is with God at the creation and is one with God, when he accepts humanity and becomes a brother (Heb. 3:1; 4:15) he is lower than the angels for a time. Later he is exalted, after his death and resurrection, to his former place and seated at the right hand, and obtains all control from God. In a sense, the same concept is operative in the Gospel accounts of the transfiguration. In Mark 8:27–9:19, for example, as a human teacher Jesus struggles to make himself understood by his disciples and others. In 9:2–8 he is shown to be superior to the greatest prophets (Moses and Elijah). Even though God declares him to be the unique Son, in a loud voice from heaven, the disciples do not know what to make of him, and when he comes down from the mountain, he is exasperated by the ineptitude of those who remained behind.

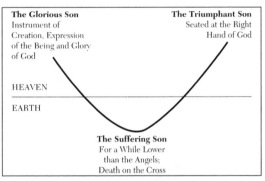

Parabola of Salvation by Thomas G. Long, *Hebrews*, 22.

One Historical Parallel

Historical circumstances also demonstrate why it is important for the author of Hebrews to insist that Jesus be understood as the Son of God with absolute power. In the Roman world, the divine nature of the emperors and emperor worship were of central importance. When Augustus was close to death without an heir, he adopted Trajan as a son and appointed him successor. After Augustus died, he was elevated to the pantheon of gods by the Roman senate, and Trajan became the "son of god." This title was given to all subsequent emperors, and Nero even claimed to be divine while he was still alive. In this context, it was important for the readers of Hebrews to know that claims by the emperors were bogus. Although Roman military might was frightening and overwhelming, ultimate power and honor was only to be found in Jesus Christ.

Transition Again

As in the case of 1:1–4, the author of Hebrews ties his sections together with obvious connections that make it possible for listeners or readers to remember what was said before and see where the line of argument is going next. Picking up on the reference to Psalm 110 in 1:4 and the mention of angels, in Hebrews 1:13 the psalm is quoted more fully to show how Jesus would be elevated to God's right hand. In the next section, angels are mentioned again (2:2, 5), and the parabola of salvation is used once more, this time with Psalm 8 as the focal point.

 Questions for Reflection

1. Which of the passages from the Hebrew Bible cited in Hebrews 1:5–14 strike you as being the most valuable in understanding Jesus' relationship to God?
2. What influences in our world today tempt us to think that they are more powerful than Jesus Christ?
3. If you were going to write in honor of Christ, what words and symbols would you use to describe him?
4. What do you think of the way the author of Hebrews uses the Hebrew Bible to prove his points? What value is it to us today? Can you understand who Jesus really is without relating him to Old Testament ideas and prophecies?

3

Jesus Christ Is Our Trailblazer

The second chapter of Hebrews is connected with previous sections, as we have seen before, by the concept of chain links and the reuse of key words. Here these literary devices emphasize the solidity of God's message:

2:1 "What we have heard"
2:2 "the message declared"   ↔ 1:1 "spoken to us by a Son"
2:12 "I will proclaim"

salvation in Jesus Christ:

2:3 "so great a salvation"   ↔ 1:14 "those who are to inherit
                                        salvation"

and the work of angels:

2:2 "the message . . . through   ↔ 1:5 "to which of the angels
    angels"   did God ever say?"
2:5 "God did not subject the   ↔ 1:7 "He makes his angels
    coming world . . . to angels"   winds"
2:9 "made lower than the angels" ↔ 1:14 "Are not all angels
                                         spirits . . . ?"

The verses of chapter 2 move beyond previous arguments to capsulize key themes that will be found throughout the rest of the sermon—namely, Jesus is higher than angels, he is our trailblazer, he is brother to those who believe, and he is the true high priest. It also introduces two central concepts for understanding the book, *sanctification* and *atonement*.

An Opening Piece of Advice

Unit 3 begins with a type of writing that will be used many other times to tip us off that a major point is about to be made, that is, the giving of spiritual and moral advice. In 13:22 the author calls it "exhortation," a word that may also be translated "teaching," "ethical imperative," "recommendations," or "warning." Normally this kind of advice is introduced with an expression or gesture designed to get the listeners to be more observant, or gives them an imperative like "*Therefore we must* pay attention" [italics added in all quotations here]; "*Therefore*, brothers and sisters, . . . *consider*" (3:1); "*Take care*, brothers and sisters" (3:12); "*Therefore*, . . . *let us* take care" (4:1); "*Since, then,* we have a great high priest, . . . *let us* hold fast" (4:14); "*Therefore, let us* go on" (6:1); "*Let us consider* how to provoke one another to love" (10:24); "*Let us run* with perseverance the race" (12:1); etc. In this case, the author wants listeners to concentrate on the messages from God that they have heard previously.

The Testimony of the Word (2:1–4)

The first call to intensified hearing is reinforced with a nautical image "so that we do not drift away." This language is found elsewhere in Hebrews where anxiety is expressed that believers might slip away from their moorings. The way for them to remain secure in spite of the storms and winds of persecution is to be anchored in God's word about Jesus Christ (6:19).

The author next pictures himself in a court of law where he must prove his case according to recognized guidelines of courtroom procedure. Since at least three consistent witnesses were required in a Jewish court to provide proper evidence, he lays out the case with five sources of expert testimony. As it is stated in 6:16, "Human beings . . . swear by someone greater than themselves, and an oath given as confirmation puts an end to all dispute."

The word that the readers have already received is true and reliable because

—the angels' message was *valid* (2:2);

—*the Lord* Jesus himself (in his ministry and through his words in the Old Testament) declared it to be true from the *first* (2:3);

—*it was attested . . . by those who heard him*, that is, his disciples and the apostles who knew what he taught;

—*God added . . . testimony by signs and wonders and various miracles* (see the discussion below) (2:4);

—The Holy Spirit guarantees it by giving spiritual gifts to the people in the church who have to preach and live it.

"Signs and wonders" is a common expression used in the Hebrew and Christian scriptures to point to symbolic actions throughout history that were given to lead the people to truth about God's power in the present and in the days to come. Some of them include the great events of salvation history, the exodus event, the miracles of the prophets, Jesus' healing and nature miracles, the powerful acts of the apostles and other members of the early church, and so on (see Deut. 4:34; 6:22; 7:19; 29:3; Jer. 32:20–21; Dan. 4:2 ; 6:27; John 4:48; Acts 2:22, 43; 4:30; 5:12; 6:8; 1 Cor. 1:22).

The gifts of the Holy Spirit are the special talents that the Holy Spirit provides for all Christians to enable them to serve the church. They are not behavioral traits that can be acquired or developed, but are bestowed at birth, according to the decision of the Spirit (see 1 Cor. 12:11). Paul indicates in Romans 12 that many of them are concerned with communication of God's word, that is, discernment, preaching, teaching, and giving spiritual advice (12:6–8). In 1 Cor. 12:4–12 oth-

Key Terms

Salvation God's rescue of humanity from sin and death to eternal life. (See Alexander, 807)

ers are listed as *utterance of knowledge, prophecy*, and *interpretation of tongues*. All of these, as he puts it, are given not for personal gratification but "for the common good" (v. 7) and the building up of the church. In Hebrews, the Spirit is a prime witness to Jesus' identity (3:7; 9:8; 10:15, 29), and it would be a terrible travesty of the truth if Christians ignored such powerful evidence and instead of receiving a "great" salvation, were justly punished for their transgressions and disobedience before God.

A New Understanding of Psalm 8

Hebrews 2:5–8 returns to the theme of Jesus' superiority over angels with a citation of Psalm 8: 4–6 as a further witness ("someone has testified somewhere," v. 6.). Although the psalmist writes in amazement about the fact that human beings are created wonderfully and are just a little lower than God (some versions read "angels"—see note h in

Ps. 8:5, NRSV), the author of Hebrews uses this Old Testament text to show that the reference is really to Jesus. It is almost as if he should not be called merely "a human being" who is lower than the angels, but "the Human Being," the Homo sapiens par excellence. After all, he reasons, salvation is not under the control of angels and is not offered for their benefit. As he puts it in 2:16, "For it is clear that he did not come to help angels, but the descendants of Abraham."

His readers need to remember that any faith in the ultimate power of angels or other heavenly beings is misplaced. Final authority is allocated only to Jesus Christ. Even though he was made *lower* than angels throughout his earthly life, particularly in his suffering and death, eventually everyone on heaven and earth will be subject to him as the *heir of all things* (1:2) when he is seated on God's right hand. It is possible that this high concept of Jesus' identity is similar to the use of the title Son of Man, which Jesus uses as a name to define himself as the one who will appear on the clouds at the last day to wrap up human history on God's behalf (see Mark 2:10; 8:31, 38; 14:21, 62; John 3:13, 14 and other Gospel passages; Acts 7:56; cf. Rev. 1:13; 14:14; Dan. 7:13 [note a, NRSV]; 8:17 [note l]; Ezek. 1:3; 2:1 [note f]; 6:2).

Who Is Abraham?

Abraham, often called the father or parent of Judaism, is a key figure in Hebrews. See 6:13, 15; 7:1–9; 11:8, 17. According to Genesis 12:1–3, by following God's command to leave his home and go to a new place, Abraham became a blessing and was made the one through whom all the nations of the earth would be blessed. Hebrews 11:8 and 17 list him as a prime example of one who lived by faith and believed in God's commands. Paul makes a similar point in Romans 4 and Galatians 3–4 where Abraham demonstrates that salvation comes not by performing works and actions but through faith in Jesus Christ. Today, Abraham's role in the founding of three major religions, Judaism, Christianity, and Islam, is an important centerpiece for international dialogue.

Everything and for All

In order to understand the scope of the power that is being attributed to Jesus, attention needs to be paid to the word *everything* in v. 8. Coming from the Greek *ta panta*, "The All," it points to his cosmic status. In some religious philosophies in the ancient world (in versions of Gnosticism, for example), it was believed that human beings would eventually be absorbed into the divine, the "All in All." In Hebrews it is Jesus himself who has this power, and this force will be his when he returns to God. As Paul puts it somewhat differently in 1 Cor. 15:28, "When all things [*ta panta*] are subjected to him, then the Son himself will also be subjected to the one who put all things in subjection under him, so that God may be all in all [*panta en pasin*]."

The expression *taste death for everyone* indicates how it will happen (Heb. 2:9). *Taste death* is a euphemism for describing the experience of dying (cf. Matt. 16:28; Mark 9:1; Luke 9:27; John 8:52) and points here to the fact that although Jesus is the true reflection of God's glory, he has to undergo terrible suffering so that God's grace and power might be revealed. "For everyone" (*huper pantos*) is defined in Hebrews 5:9 as "all who obey him," those for whom Jesus is the "source of eternal salvation." Compare Mark 10:45 where Jesus says that the Son of Man came to give his life as a ransom for many.

Trailblazer, Brother, High Priest

In Hebrews 1 the titles for Jesus are kept at the highest level to demonstrate that he is in direct contact with God, that is, the Son, the reflection of God's glory, the imprint of God's very being. In 2:10–18 three new names are introduced that provide mixed metaphors to describe who Jesus really is: one that is practical and strategic (*pioneer*), another that is personal and intimate (*brother*), and the final one, religious and political (*high priest*).

The word *pioneer* (it could also be translated "trailblazer" or "guide") is unusual in the New Testament and is found only in Hebrews, Acts 3:15 ("Author of life"), and Acts 5:31 ("Leader"). Here and in Hebrews 12:2, it is used in similar contexts picturing Jesus as a leader who goes before others on a dangerous path, being willing to suffer and even die so that followers may be safe. For Jesus, the road that must be traveled is the one mentioned in the Gospels and Acts—it is the *way* of the Lord that leads to the cross (Mark 1:2–3; 10: 32, 52), and it is also the name even given to those who follow him, the people of *the Way* (Acts 9:2; 16:17; 18:26; 19:23; 22:4; 24:14).

> **A Pioneer Faith**
>
> My faith is simple
> like a log cabin floor,
> varnished clear
> by years of use.
> No complex joints
> hold it together
> with nails and synthetic glue.
> You can stand on it.
> And that's that.
> Earl S. Johnson, Jr.

It is possible to think back to colonial days to provide an example of what is meant here. In the area of New York State northwest of Albany, there is a road that is called "the Nick Stoner Trail." Stoner was a hunter and a trapper, a scout during the Revolutionary War, and an explorer and a mountain man in his later years. People still like to follow his path from the Mohawk River north through Johnstown, up to Caroga Lake into the Adirondacks, imagining that they still have his adventurous and independent spirit. Somewhat similarly, Hebrews provides the image of Jesus as the one who breaks trail for believers today.

Want to Know More

About questions people raise about angels today? See Luke Timothy Johnson, *Hebrews: A Commentary*, New Testament Library (Louisville, Ky.: Westminster John Knox Press, 2006), 82–84.

About the structural importance of the exhortation sections in Hebrews? See Cynthia Long Westfall, *A Discourse Analysis of the Letter to the Hebrews, The Relationship between Form and Meaning* (London: T. & T. Clark, 2005).

About the role of the high priest in Judaism and Christianity? See Helen K. Bond, *Caiaphas: Friend of Rome and Judge of Jesus?* (Louisville, Ky.: Westminster John Knox Press, 2004).

The second image of Jesus, in Hebrews 2:11–13, is much more personal. Citing Psalm 22:22, the author claims that Jesus is so close to Christians that he is willing to suffer for them and call them *brothers and sisters* (literally *brothers* in Greek). He is able to connect this text with the concept of Jesus' willingness to suffer for the sins of the world because it is the very same psalm that Jesus quotes on the cross when he is about to die (Mark 15:34; Matt. 27:46). Elsewhere other New Testament writers assert that all those who believe in Christ as Lord and Savior are children of God along with him (John 1:12–13; 1 John 2:1, 18, 28). As it is put in 1 John 3:1, "See what love the Father has given us, that we should be called children of God; and that is what we are."

The author of Hebrews can say that his listeners are brothers and sisters of Jesus because

— they are children of God and Jesus is the Son;
— they have the same heavenly Parent (the Father);
— they have the same genealogy, since Abraham, the father of the nations, is their mutual ancestor;
— they suffer hardship in this world, but Jesus has gone ahead of them to prepare the way;
— since all human beings must die sometime, Jesus came in *flesh and blood* (Heb. 2:14) so he could overcome death on their behalf;
— Jesus became part of the human family so that he could be in solidarity with all those who must suffer. "He had to become like his brothers and sisters in every respect. . . . Because he himself was tested by what he suffered, he is able to help those who are being tested." (2:17–18)

In the final title applied to Jesus in this chapter, it is said that Jesus is a *merciful and faithful high priest in the service of God* (2:17), a name that will be utilized frequently in the rest of the letter throughout chapters 3–10 and in 13:11. Much more will be said about its significance in those contexts, but here it is worth noting that the high priest was the head of the Jerusalem Temple and the political and spiritual leader of the Jewish government.

Although he was appointed by the king in the first century CE, he still had tremendous power and was the only priest who could enter the Holy of Holies in Herod's Temple on the Day of Atonement (Yom Kippur). It was the high priest Caiaphas who tried Jesus and turned him over to Pilate to be crucified (Mark 14:53–65 and parallels).

In Hebrews it is asserted that the power of the high priest is ended. Atonement is no longer accomplished by the sacrifice of animals in Jerusalem, but by the death of Jesus. Jesus not only replaces the high priest; he is the high priest. He not only offers the sacrifice for the people; he is the sacrifice. He does not enter the presence of God in the Temple; he is that very presence personified (Heb. 10:1–25).

Key Terms

Sanctification The way a believer is made holy; how new life is imparted by the Holy Spirit to make service to God and love of the neighbor possible

Atonement The process by which the broken relationship between God and human beings is restored to oneness through the death and resurrection of Jesus Christ, often called "at-one-ment" (Harvey, 1964.)

? Questions for Reflection

1. Exhortation, the giving of spiritual advice, is still part of preaching in churches today. Can you think of any recent sermons in which your pastor has urged your members toward a specific kind of behavior?
2. If Jesus Christ is our brother, how can we express the fact that the church really is family?
3. Who were the pioneers, the founding mothers and fathers, in your congregation? How were they influenced by the example of Jesus Christ?
4. Stories appear in the news occasionally about family members giving one of their kidneys to save a loved one who is on dialysis. How does this willingness to suffer on behalf of another person relate to the Christian doctrine of the atonement through Jesus Christ?

4 Hebrews 3:1–4:13

Jesus Christ Is Greater than Faith's Founders

The discussion about Jesus' superiority over all powers and beings in heaven and on earth is brought closer to home as readers are moved from angels in the heavenly courts and the power of the high priest to the central Old Testament image of the prophet Moses and his role leading the people of God out of Egypt.

Moses and Jesus

This section begins with a comparison and contrast between Jesus and Moses. For Jews and Christians, Moses is often considered the paragon of faith, the founder of Judaism and the George Washington of the nation of Israel. According to the Old Testament, he survived a dangerous birth in Egypt, was rescued from the bulrushes by Pharaoh's daughter, and was eventually brought up as the ruler's adopted son. When he discovered what was happening to the Hebrew people, who were locked in oppressive slavery, he fled from Egypt and was called by God to set his people free. The story of Moses' work of liberation, the forty-year sojourn across the Sinai, his transmittal of the Ten Commandments from Mount Sinai, and his preparation of the people to enter the promised land establish him as a primary political and spiritual figure in Old and New Testament faith.

The author of Hebrews joins other New Testament writers who saw Moses as a predecessor and forerunner of Jesus. When Jesus gives the Sermon on the Mount (Matt. 5–7), he is reinterpreting the law of God for a new time. When he meets Moses and Elijah on the Mount of Transfiguration, God establishes Jesus' priority over these leaders as the unique Son (Matt. 17:1–13; Mark 9:2–13; Luke 9:28–36). Paul pictures the Christian life as a new exodus (1 Cor. 10), and Revelation 15:3–8 proclaims that at the end time the angels will sing the song of Moses, the servant of God, and the song of the Lamb.

In Hebrews 3:2 the author compares Jesus to this great leader when he writes that Jesus was faithful to the one who appointed him just as Moses was faithful to the God who called him to set his people free (Exod. 3; see Num. 12:7). In Hebrews 3:5 Moses is described as one who points to the future as he prepares the people for the coming of Christ: "Now Moses was faithful in all God's house as servant, to testify to the things that would be spoken later." The idea is

Moses Breaking the Tablets of the Law, Exodus by Gustave Dore (1832–83) (after)

expressed somewhat similarly by Jesus in John 5:46, "If you believed Moses, you would believe me, for he wrote about me," and in his parable about the rich man and Lazarus, "If they do not listen to Moses and the prophets, neither will they be convinced even if someone rises from the dead" (Luke 16:31).

Apostle of Our Confession

Hebrews takes the comparison between Jesus and Moses to another level when it is said that Jesus is superior to the one who prepared the way for him because he is the apostle and high priest of our confession. The word *apostle* supports the claim that Jesus was faithful to his appointment by God (Heb. 3:2) because it means "one who is sent," that is, a messenger or ambassador from a king or other important person. In this case Jesus is given a title as God's diplomat, one who speaks on God's behalf, a plenipotentiary who communicates for the One who sent him. The prophets often filled this role when they were given the responsibility for conveying God's message to the people.

Jesus is better than the prophets and Moses, however, because he is more than an emissary from God—he is God's Son. *Apostle* is also used to describe the first Christians called to proclaim the good news of Jesus Christ, and was limited to those who had received their commission directly from him after the resurrection (see the discussion in Gal. 1–2 for an example). This is the only place where Jesus is given this title, and it may indicate that if he is greater than Moses he is also greater than the church's apostles whose power comes directly from him (Mark 3:14; Acts 1:2).

The *confession* of which he is the apostle is not merely a message, furthermore, but a certified statement of the truth that God wishes to transmit. Confession in this context does not mean the prayer for forgiveness used in worship, but creedal statements like the Apostles' Creed, or the powerful Old Testament statement of faith where the people are commanded to love God with their whole heart, mind, and strength (Deut. 6:4–6). To "confess" in Greek literally means to "say the same thing," to "acknowledge," to "declare publicly," and points to a statement of belief about Jesus Christ as Lord and Savior (see Heb. 13:15). Paul says, for example, that every tongue should confess that Jesus is Lord, to the glory of God (Phil. 2:11), and that a statement of belief that God raised him from the dead leads to salvation (Rom. 10:9–10). In 1 Timothy 6:12 "the good confession" is mentioned, which is made in the presence of many witnesses (see other references in Rom. 10:10; 2 Cor. 9:13; 1 John 2:23; 4:3). In Hebrews such a statement of faith is one that provides hope (3:6), confidence (4:14), and the assurance of Jesus' faithfulness (10:23).

Want to Know More?

About questions about the historicity of Moses? See "Moses," in *The HarperCollins Bible Dictionary*, ed. Paul J. Achtemeier (San Francisco: HarperSanFrancisco, 1996), 708.

House of God (3:1–6)

In 3:1–6 the author moves beyond the person of Moses to discuss the significance of the Exodus for Christian readers. He does this with the introduction of the metaphor of the house. This connection is based primarily on Numbers 12:6–7, where it is said that although God speaks to prophets in visions and dreams, he communicates with Moses face to face because "he is entrusted with all my house." In Hebrews *house* has several levels of meaning. It stands as a symbol of the "house of God," the place where people meet with God, the location of the tent of meeting in the wilderness (Exod. 23:19; 34:26; 1 Kings 6:1; 8:20; Ps. 27:4). More generally, it can refer to the people of God who are faithful, God's family, living and acting together under one spiritual roof (see Acts 2:36). As Moses' successor, Joshua puts it at the end of his ministry: "Now if you are unwilling to serve the LORD, choose this day whom who will serve . . . ; but as for me and my household, we will serve the LORD" (Josh. 24:15).

In the New Testament the concept is especially connected with Jesus' ministry. He often teaches and heals in a house, a location of safety, intimacy, and revelation (see Mark 1:29; 2:15; 9:33; 10:10). When he cleanses the outer courtyard of the Jerusalem Temple of money changers, he despairs that it is no longer treated as the house of God (Mark 11:17; cf. Isa. 56:5–7). Since the early church started out on a small scale, furthermore, without a great deal of money or prestige, congregations literally worshiped in the homes of members (Acts 2:2; 8:3; 9:17; 12:12; Rom. 16:5; 1 Cor. 16:19; Col. 4:15). According to tradition, a house church met in the home of Peter in Capernaum, and archaeological evidence indicates that a church building existed on that site for centuries after his death. Later "house" became a cipher for the entire Christian movement (Heb. 3:6; 8:8, 10; 10:21; 1 Pet. 2:5; 4:17).

In Hebrews 3:1–6 the concept is extended in architectural terms to show why Jesus is better than Moses. If the real designer and builder of the house of faith is God, it only makes sense that the builder's own Son is better than one who serves in it as a servant (Moses).

Exodus and the Concept of Rest (3:7–4:11)

In Hebrews 3:7–4:11 a fairly long illustration of the central significance of the exodus is given, in which Psalm 95 serves as a critical passage to help readers understand the spiritual concept of *rest*. Recapitulating the story of the forty years of wandering in the Sinai (see Exod. 13:18–40:38; the accounts in Numbers and Deuteronomy; Josh. 1:1–9), the author focuses on the *hardness of heart* of the people (see question 1 below), the time of testing, and the fact they could not enter God's rest until after Moses' death.

In this passage *rest* has many facets. It can refer to the concept of God's resting after the first six days of creation (Heb. 4:4; Gen. 2:2) and the development of the Jewish observance of the seventh day as a

Sabbath of worship and cessation from work (Exod. 20:8–11; 31:12–17). It also signifies an understanding of what occurred during the forty years of wandering and the reason why the people of God never reached the spiritual state they desired. Because they disobeyed God, because they did not trust in God's direction, because they hardened their hearts and turned away to other gods, even when they entered the promised land under Joshua, they still did not achieve the fullness of what was intended for them. Thus in Hebrews 4:9 it can be said that "a sabbath rest still remains for the people of God."

Because the names Joshua and Jesus are spelled the same in Greek (*Iesous*, "one who saves"), New Testament writers saw a close connection between the two (Heb. 4:8; Acts 7:45). In some texts of Jude 5 (see footnote f, NRSV), it is said that *Jesus* was actually the one who led the people out of Egypt.

Who Is Joshua?

The successor of Moses (Num. 27:18–23; Deut. 3:28; 31:23), Joshua was the leading military leader in the conquest of Canaan. He also organized reconnaissance missions before the armies crossed the Jordan River (Num. 13:1–16; 14:6–9; Josh. 2). The accounts about his invasions have been examined carefully by historians and archaeologists, and there is a great deal of debate about the historicity of the book of Joshua. (See Richard D. Nelson, 2–5).

The author of Hebrews uses this concept to indicate how sin, a basic attitude of rebellion against God's love and a defiant rejection of the commandments of God, leads to spiritual unrest and eventual death (Deut. 30:15–20; Rom. 6:23). In this sense, even Moses did not provide adequate *leadership* (Heb. 3:16) of the house of God, and by his own example prevented them from realizing the truth. Because he also had disobeyed God himself, he was punished and was not allowed to enter the land of Canaan but had to look at it from afar.

In Hebrews 3:1–4:11 the central story in the Jewish faith of the exodus is used to show why the covenant between God and the people cannot be realized without Christ. The point of the sermon here is introduced in 3:13, where listeners are encouraged not to repeat the mistake that the Israelites made in the wilderness, "But exhort one another every day, as long as it is called 'today,' so that none of you may be hardened by the deceitfulness of sin." Unbelief, he indicates, can keep us from God (3:19). "Let us therefore make every effort to enter that rest, so that no one may fall through such disobedience as theirs" (4:11). The same idea is developed by Paul in 1 Cor. 10: 9–12, "We must not put Christ to the test, as some of them did. . . . And do not complain as some of them did. . . . These things happened to them to serve as an example, and they were written down to instruct us, on whom the ends of the ages have come. So if you think you are standing, watch out that you do not fall."

The concept *today* in Hebrews 3:13; 4:7, 8 is taken from Ps. 95:7 and points to the necessity of an immediate decision. Turning to God is not something that should be put off. If one waits too long, it could be too late.

The Penetrating Power of the Word (4:12–13)

The final paragraph in this section reconnects with 1:3 (God's powerful word) with a new metaphor to describe the word of God. In a familiar passage that is often used in prayers of illumination in our contemporary worship, "the word of God is living and active, sharper than any two-edged sword," reference is made to the ability of God's message to expose all pretenses. Obviously, this military image would have been graphically uncomfortable to the original readers. Every day they had the opportunity to see Roman soldiers intimidate them and their neighbors with the double-bladed weapon that could maim and kill, and the reference here would remind them of the dangerous political reality they could not escape. For early Christians the sword also served as a symbol of a prophet's warning (Isa. 49:2) or the judgment of God (Rev. 1:16; 19:15, 21).

Today we might make the same point using the somewhat different terms of a modern hospital operating room. Surgical tools and lasers open successive layers of the body of the patient, and various organs are revealed as the operation proceeds. The author of Hebrews somewhat similarly imagines the precision of God as it separates believers from their rationalizations, cuts out the malignancies that could lead to death, and removes the spiritual arteriosclerosis (hardness of heart) that threatens continuing spiritual life. God is like the skilled surgeon who is not deceived by false appearances of wellness and knows exactly what radical procedures are necessary to restore health.

? Questions for Reflection

1. The concept of sinful behavior leading to a spiritual condition called "hardness of heart" appears often in the New Testament (see Mark 3:5; 6:52; 8:17; 10:5; John 12:40; Rom. 9:18; 11:5, 7; Eph.

4:18). Do you see any examples of it in your church or in American society today?

2. In Hebrews 3:1 and 3:14 it is said that believers are "partners of a heavenly calling" and "partners in Christ." The basic meaning points to a spiritual sharing (see 6:4; 12:8). In what ways do Christians share with one another as the Holy Spirit leads them?

3. Throughout Hebrews it is said that the *promise* (4:1) of God was not received fully by anyone until Christ came and made it *better* (8:6; also see 6:12, 15; 10:36; 11:9,13, 33, 39). How would you define this promise and how is it realized in him?

4. The Greek word "turning away" in 3:12 is the root of the English word "apostasy." What would it mean to desert or depart from *the living God* today?

Jesus Christ Is Greater than the Highest Religious Leaders

Hard to Understand

Many readers of this section will find the author's somewhat enigmatic disclaimer in Hebrews 5:11 ("About this we have much to say that is hard to explain") somewhat comforting since it is certainly not easy for most of us to comprehend the images and line of reasoning he uses in this section. The complexity is due to the centrality of the mysterious figure of Melchizedek throughout, an Old Testament personage who is mentioned only here in the entire New Testament. When the author's logic is outlined in some detail, however, and the function of Melchizedek in other Jewish literature is understood, the purpose of 4:14–7:28 becomes clearer, and we begin to view the shape of a message that was important in its original context and is still valuable to the church today.

> It is solid food indeed: The argument is elaborate and complex, and modern Christians are likely to find its ancient logic bewildering and difficult to digest! Still, we may appreciate the author's stunning conclusions and the innovation in early Christian thinking that they represent. (Gench, 41)

The Argument about Melchizedek

The argument in these verses that Jesus is an eternal high priest because he comes from the line of Melchizedek is the most difficult one in Hebrews, and ranks among the most complex in the whole New Testament. It is made especially incomprehensible for modern readers because it uses a kind of imagery called "typology" that is not easy to understand today. New Testament writers often argue that if you can find a connection between Christ and an Old Testament passage or personage, you have demonstrated the truth about Jesus' Sonship, or Messiahship. In Romans 5:14, for example, Paul says that Adam is "a type of the one who was to come," that is, that Adam was the forerunner of Jesus. In a sense they are saying, "If it is in the Old Testament, it must be so." Today we can marvel at the way God inspired Old Testament prophets, be impressed with the prescience of writers as they looked ahead, and find ourselves interested in the similarities between Jesus and Moses, Adam, or Melchizedek, but we are not automatically convinced by proof texts or easily persuaded that close comparisons necessarily point to incontrovertible evidence that there is a definite spiritual connection.

> **Who were the Levites?**
>
> According to Deuteronomy 10:8, they were set apart by the Lord to carry the Ark of the Covenant and organize worship as the priests of the people. See Joshua 14:4; 2 Chronicles 31:2; 34:9; 35:3–6.

In order to appreciate the point being made about Melchizedek in Hebrews 4:14–7:28 it is helpful to track the author's logic so we can see how his thinking proceeds.

A [1] The Jewish high priest offered animal sacrifices on the Day of Atonement for the forgiveness of sins (5:1–4).

B [1] Jesus is a high priest too, but not through a historical lineage (7:13–17). Since he comes through the eternal order of Melchizedek, he is a superior high priest, one who offers himself as sacrifice (5:5–6).

A [2] Since the high priest was human in every respect, he was subject to all weaknesses (i.e., sin, 5:2) and even had to offer sacrifices for himself.

B [2] Jesus suffered as we do and was tempted as we are (5:7–9) but without sin (7:27). Therefore, he is a better high priest, one who is holy, blameless, and undefiled (7:26).

A [3] The priesthood of the people came through Levi and Aaron, through the Levitical line.

B [3] Jesus came through Melchizedek, and since Melchizedek was superior to Aaron, Jesus is better (5:4; 7:11–14).

A [4] High priests get their authority through physical descent and legal succession, but since they all die, there are many of them throughout history (7:16, 23).

B **4** Jesus has been called through an eternal priesthood, and since God raised him from the dead, he is eternally superior, "a priest forever" (5:6; 6:20; 7:3, 16, 24–25), and his sacrifice is *once for all* (7:27) and *perfect* (7:28).

Background of Melchizedek

Although Melchizedek does not appear elsewhere in the New Testament, recent studies demonstrate that he was a key figure in Jewish and Christian expectations about the future, and that first-century readers were likely to have been familiar with speculations about his importance in God's plans for the coming age.

In the Dead Sea Scrolls (documents written before the birth of Jesus), for example, an eschatological writing called *11 Q Melchizedek* indicates that "the inheritance of Melchizedek" assures the Jews that they will be able to return to their homeland and that he will bring them liberty from the ravages of the evil one (Belial). In a later text found in Nag Hammadi (Egypt), he similarly appears to play a role in the Jews' salvation. In 2 Enoch 72, a rabbinic text of uncertain date (possibly first century CE), he is said to have been protected as a child by the archangel Gabriel and was designated by God to become "the originator of the priests" in later generations. In other writings, the Jewish historian Flavius Josephus (ca. 37–100 CE) emphasizes his priestly role, his relationship with Abraham, and the connection of Salem with the city of Jerusalem (*Ant.* 1.10.2). Philo Judaeus (ca. 13 BCE–50 CE), a prominent Jewish theologian and philosopher from Alexandria, carefully develops the allegorical implications of Melchizedek's place as the high priest of God, emphasizing his righteousness and the fact that his thoughts about God were high, vast, and sublime. (See Luke Timothy Johnson for references, 176–77, 181–83.) These texts demonstrate that Hebrews was not written in a vacuum but that the author was drawing on imagery already familiar to his readers.

In the Old Testament, on the other hand, references to Melchizedek appear only in two places, in Genesis 14:17–24 and in Psalm 110:4. In Hebrews 6:13–7:17 the author uses these passages to show his superiority to all other priests. For him, the Genesis account

> **Who is Aaron?**
>
> The brother of Moses (Exod. 4:14–17; 7:1–2), he was chosen to be the spokesperson for both of them (Exod. 4:14–16). He was one of the descendants of Levi (Exod. 28) and founded the line of priests after the exodus.

demonstrates that since Abraham, the founder of the Hebrew nation, paid a tribute (a tithe) to Melchizedek (7:4–6) and needed to be blessed by him (7:6), Melchizedek obviously outranks him since "it is beyond dispute that the inferior is blessed by the superior" (7:7). Melchizedek can even be seen to be preeminent over Levi, the founder of the priestly line, since Abraham was, in a manner of speaking, Levi's forefather because "he was still in the loins of his ancestor" (7:10). We might say that Levi was already in Abraham's DNA.

Want to Know More?

About Melchizedek? See Luke Timothy Johnson, *Hebrews*, Excursus 4, "The Mysterious Melchizedek," (Louisville, Ky.: Westminster John Knox Press, 2006), 181–83; Harold Attridge, *The Epistle to the Hebrews*, Hermeneia (Philadelphia: Fortress Press, 1989), 192–94.

In chapter 7 the author places special emphasis on the mysterious background of Melchizedek in order to highlight the distance between the Levitical high priests and Jesus as the true high priest. Arguing that Melchizedek means "king of righteousness" in Hebrew and that *Salem* is the word for "peace" (7:1–2), he suggests that even the names used to describe this king indicate the primacy given to him by God. Since no background information is supplied about Melchizedek in the Old Testament, he is able to attribute to him an origin that takes on a somewhat superhuman, mythological, and eternal status: "Without father, without mother, without genealogy, having neither beginning of days nor end of life, but resembling the Son of God, he remains a priest forever" (7:3). In this latter assertion he buttresses his argument in 5:6–7 with a quotation from Psalm 110:4, a psalm that he has used before to refer to Christ (see Heb. 1:13): "You are a priest forever, according to the order of Melchizedek."

For the original readers of Hebrews, many of them converts from Judaism, this argument must have been good news. They would have felt the freedom that is offered in chapters 8–13, when it is made clear that, because of Melchizedek, Old Testament methods of animal sacrifice no longer needed to be practiced. All these things have been supplanted by the one for whom Melchizedek was a forerunner, the one who is "the mediator of a better covenant, which has been enacted through better promises" (8:6).

The Humanity of Jesus

For modern readers the emphasis in this section on the elevated status of Jesus as eternal high priest may give us hope that the sacrifice of his death has secured God's promise of forgiveness for all time—not just in the first century, not just in our day and age, but for all eternity (see 9:26–31). But another aspect of the description of Jesus' Sonship may be even more moving for believers today, that is, the touching descriptions of his humanity.

In 4:15, for example, the section begins with a reference to the fact that Jesus is able to sympathize (*sumpatheo* in Greek) with our sinfulness (*weaknesses*), having been tested in every way as we are. This sympathy comes from his own temptation by Satan before his ministry began (Matt. 4:1–11; Mark 1:12–13; Luke 4:1–13), his general experiences as a human being, and by the taunts thrown at him by opponents (Matt. 22:18; Mark 12:15; John 8:6). Jesus understands the trials that believers face because he has been through them himself. The fact that he was willing to die for the sins of others becomes even more poignant when it is recognized that he did so *without sin* (Heb. 4:15).

A similar expression of Jesus' empathy is found in 5:7, where it is said that as a human being (*in the days of his flesh*), Jesus understandably agonized over the suffering he had to face on the cross and *offered up prayers and supplications, with loud cries and tears, to the one who was able to save him from death*. Certainly this reference to his agony in the Garden of Gethsemane (Matt. 26:36–56; Mark 14:32–42; Luke 22:39–46) is intended to recall his grief and his prayer to God that he be delivered from torture and death, if God willed it. It graphically reminds Christians of the suffering we sometimes experience when we witness to our faith or are determined to do God's will regardless of the consequences. In such a circumstance, as the author of Hebrews reminds us, we have a *forerunner* (Heb. 6:20, see the comments elsewhere on Jesus as the *pioneer*, Units 3 and 10) who can help us in every time of need (4:16).

Some Tough Pastoral Advice (5:11–14, 6:1–12)

This very human aspect of Jesus' message and ministry is also expressed in 5:11–14 and chapter 6 where the author deals with some concrete pastoral concerns. The problem appears to be that some of his readers have fallen to temptation and are in danger of losing their faith. His anxiety stems from the fact that they do not seem to be making any progress in essential Christian learning and have *become dull in understanding* (5:11). Even though they have been believers long enough to be teachers themselves, they still desperately need someone to teach them the basic elements of the faith. Their understanding of Christian principles is so elementary that they are like whining babies who need milk (5:12) or some kind of infant formula to sustain them when they already have enough mature theological teeth to chew on real food. As Paul says in 1 Corinthians 3:2, "I fed you with milk, not solid food, for you were not ready for solid food. Even now you are still not ready."

In chapter 6 the author of Hebrews warns that readers are in real danger if they fail to advance to maturity. They should not continue to debate aspects of faith that he considers elementary, such as the basic issues of repentance ("Am I saved?"), concepts of baptism, arguments about resurrection of the dead (compare 1 Cor. 15:12, "How can some of you say there is no resurrection of the dead?"), and the nature of final judgment, as if they were still catechumens or members of a confirmation class. Instead, they should worry about the more serious possibility of apostasy, that is, a faith that becomes so distorted that it cannot be restored (Heb. 6:4–6). Similar warnings are given in 10:26–31, where the fearful prospect of God's judgment is graphically portrayed, and in 12:15: "See to it that no one fails to obtain the grace of God."

Although Christians today may worry that they might unwittingly fall into the kind of behavior that is being described here, that is, one beyond the power of God's forgiveness, this is not what is in mind in our passage. More to the point, the unbelief that is being discussed is the kind that is described by Jesus as the blasphemy of the Holy Spirit, the unforgivable sin (Mark 3:28–30). This rebellion against God is not accidental or inadvertent, but is a conscious rejection of God's love that is so deliberate that one chooses to reject forgiveness in Christ and, in a sense, crucifies him over and over again (Heb. 6:6). Because it wants to distort the truth, God is no longer able to penetrate the defensive ramparts that recalcitrant sin builds. As it is put in Hebrews 10:29, 31, it will be a fearful thing for those who have spurned the Son of God and outraged the Spirit of grace to fall into the hands of a living God.

Fortunately this is not the prospect faced by the first readers of Hebrews or by Christians in general today. As the author says in 6:9–12, he is confident that they have not slipped so far, and he knows that they can still find the better things of salvation (6:9). God knows that they have shown Christ's love in their work on his behalf (presumably in their witness to the truth and their concern for the poor), and his words are meant to provoke them out of sluggishness (6:12) so they can move on to true spiritual productivity (see 6:7–8). Despite the warnings in 4:14–7:28, the author continually provides a consistent word of hope. Jesus, he contends, is the source of eternal salvation, no matter what (5:9). We have the full assurance of hope until the end (6:1), an anchor in the midst of storms (6:19), a better covenant through which we can always approach God (7:18–19). Unlike the sacrifices of the high priests, Jesus' sacrifice does not need to be repeated. It is *once for all* and brings us forgiveness forever (7:27; 9:12). "And it is by God's will that we have been sanctified through the offering of the body of Jesus Christ once for all" (10:10).

? Questions for Reflection

1. What do you think about the use of Melchizedek to explain Jesus' superiority as a high priest? Does it make sense to you?
2. What does it mean to you as a Christian that Jesus suffered so much in the Garden of Gethsemane and on the cross?
3. If you were going to describe the humanity of Jesus to a child, what aspects of his life and personality would you emphasize?
4. Do you think it is ever possible for a believer to fall away from God's love and forgiveness?

6 Hebrews 8

Jesus Christ Provides
the More Excellent Ministry

The Main Point

Years ago a friend of mine (who was a Roman Catholic priest) and I liked to debate complex issues of theology. When he wanted to make a strong emphasis, he would gesture powerfully with his finger and say, "The point is . . . , the point is . . . , the point is . . . ." In a way, the introduction to chapter 8 has a similar annoying sense of repetition when the author introduces his argument with the words "Now the main point in what we are saying is this," as if readers did not get it already. Yet it is necessary to understand that as a preacher and a teacher he was aware of the fact that not every listener and reader is always paying strict attention all the time, and so he returns to fundamental concepts to make sure that no one misses them.

In fact, this kind of obvious verbal or literary device is used nowhere else in the New Testament, with the possible exception of Mark 13:14, where a key point is made about identifying important signs of the new age when the author writes "let the reader understand." In Hebrews 8:1 the first Greek word in the sentence is *kephalion*. It is related to the word *kephalos* ("head") and means the chief point or the main idea. Sometimes it is translated "In brief," "In summary." Chapter 8 serves as a kind of center point for the letter, therefore, where the author not only reminds readers of the high concept of Jesus in 1:3–4, who sits at the right hand of the Majesty on high and makes purification for sin, but also prepares them to move forward to what is coming next.

The expression "we have such a high priest" in v. 1 links future arguments to the concept of Jesus as a heavenly high priest who perfectly

38

fulfills the law (introduced in 4:14), and is developed in detail in chapters 5–7. But that is not the whole main point. As 8:6–7 reiterates, the point is, as 1:4, 6:9, and 7:19 have already indicated, the point is that Jesus is more than another high priest; he is always superior to any predecessors on earth or in heaven. The point is, as 8:6 and 7 illustrate, that Jesus is always better, since "he is the mediator of a better covenant" that has been enacted through "better promises." As it is summarized in v. 7, if the first covenant and its representatives had been perfect, "there would have been no need to look for a second one."

The True Ministry

In vv. 2–5 attention focuses again on descriptions of Jesus as high priest and on expanded interpretations of his priestly role. Defining some of the vocabulary will help us understand where the argument is going.

True tent, for example, refers to the tent of meeting, sometimes translated "tabernacle," which was constructed by the Jews during the time of the exodus wanderings (see Exod. 25–40) to house the Ark of the Covenant, the altar of incense, the seven-branched candlestick, and the bread of Presence of God (Exod. 25:30). It traveled with the people and was erected (see Heb. 8:5) wherever camp was made (Num. 1:51–53). Prior to the building of Solomon's Temple in Jerusalem, it was the chief place for worship and the reception of messages from God. The fact that worship was centered around a tent points to the original nomadic existence of the people. The imagery continued to be used in the New Testament when Christians wrote about the Word of God tenting with believers (John 1:14) or the concept of God dwelling with them forever in the life to come (Rev. 21:3).

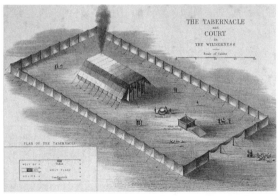

Tabernacle and Court in the Wilderness (Solomon's Temple), 19th century, litho

In Hebrews the author contrasts the original tent of meeting with the *true tent* that was not pitched by human beings, but by Jesus himself. This second tent is not one made of animal skins and held up with ropes and poles, but is a spiritual dwelling that will stand forever. He will refer to this tent repeatedly in later chapters (9:2, 3, 6, 8, 21; 13:10) and will allude to it in 10:19–22 when he discusses the veil of the temple.

In 8:5 it is indicated that the original tent of meeting is inferior to the new one Jesus establishes because it is merely *a sketch and shadow of the heavenly one*. Although the word *shadow* can describe the image cast by a person or object standing in the sun (Mark 4:32; Acts 5:15), here it refers more symbolically to an appearance that is not reality. In Colossians 2:17, for example, Paul refers to food regulations that are only a shadow of what is to come. They are illusory, for true substance belongs only to Christ. Here, in Hebrews 8:5, use is made of a well-known literary reference from Plato's *Republic*, in which those who are in a cave see only shadows on the walls rather than the actual objects outside. In such a way, the author integrates images and concepts from the intellectual culture in which readers actually live so they can understand scriptural ideas in reference to their own thought world (see introduction, p. 2). Somewhat similarly, *sketch* refers to a model or pattern used to make an object. Here it points to the fact that the tent of meeting was really merely a copy or imitation of the eternal temple of God, the one that Moses is presumed to have mentioned in Exodus 25:40: "See that you make [everything] accord to the pattern . . . ," that is, according to God's own schematics.

Want to Know More?

About the heavenly temple and its significance in Jewish thought?

See Harold W. Attridge, *The Epistle to the Hebrews*, Hermeneia (Philadelphia: Fortress Press, 1989), 222–23.

In these verses the author returns to his elaboration of Jesus' priestly role, already discussed above in Units 3 and 5 (pp. 22–23, 31–34 above). In the period during the exodus the priests carried out ritual roles of animal sacrifice and other kinds of worship. After the conquest of Palestine, sacrificial rites were no longer performed in the tent of meeting but in temples scattered throughout the nation. During the reforms of King Josiah (ca. 640–609 BCE) mentioned in Deuteronomy, all worship was centered in Jerusalem, and outlying temples were banned. After the return from exile (around 520–515 BCE), these services were performed in the Second Temple, built by Ezra and Nehemiah, and later in the one constructed by King Herod on the same site (destroyed in 70 CE). In these locations, generally speaking, in addition to ritual duties, priests were charged with other responsibilities as judges, verifying healing from diseases and supervising purification standards (see Mark 7:1–23) and the maintenance of the temple. During the Hellenistic period (142–63 BCE), the high priest had a great deal of spiritual and political power, and the office was handed down within the priestly families. Later, when King Herod (27–4 BCE) assumed a more secular kingship, he appointed the high priest. After his death the power of appointment was assumed by the Roman procurator or prefect.

If Hebrews was written after the destruction of the Temple and the capture of Jerusalem in 70 CE by the Roman army, it is not difficult to see why the author of Hebrews would emphasize how the respect for the priestly office not only *could* be transferred to Jesus, but *should* be. As he attempts to demonstrate, the fall of the priesthood is part of God's plan, and Jesus is called to fulfill all duties of the high priest, and even becomes the sacrifice that atonement requires.

In Hebrews 8:2 he emphasizes the highly spiritual function that Jesus now assumes when he calls him *a minister in the sanctuary*. The Greek word for "minister" is *leitourgos* (compare the English "liturgy"), and indicates not only Jesus' ceremonial function but his position as a servant of God (see Rom. 15:16, where the same word is used) and his pastoral concern. As v. 6 points out, his *ministry (leitourgias)* is defined by the fact that he stands as the ultimate *mediator* between God and human beings. In this central role he prays for those who follow him (cf. John 17) and brings the promised eternal inheritance (Heb. 9:15) as well as the forgiveness of the living God (Heb. 12:24). As it is stated in 1 Timothy 2:5–6, "There is one God; there is also one mediator between God and humankind, Christ Jesus, himself human, who gave himself a ransom for all."

One more aspect of Jesus' function as God's true priest is also worth noting. In his commentary on Hebrews, Craig Koester points out that more than the Jerusalem Temple may be in mind (pp. 381f.) in chapter 8. Temples were prominent places of worship in all major religions of the first century CE throughout large cities. Emperor Augustus, for example, restored eighty-two in the Roman Empire and built thirteen new ones to Apollo, Jupiter, Minerva, and Julius Caesar (called the son of God). As Koester points out, it is very likely that the readers of Hebrews assume not only that Jesus is the new high priest of Judaism but that he is the high priest for all religions in the world. It is not only the Temple in Jerusalem that is to be replaced by him. He will be the center of true worship for every religion, in every nation, and in every age—the one who is, and was, and is to be.

A Key Biblical Image: Jeremiah's New Covenant

In 8:8–12 Hebrews makes use of one of one of the most important biblical prophecies in Jewish and Christian faith, Jeremiah's prediction that a time will come when God will make a brand-new covenant with the people of God. Here and in later chapters the author draws on this magnificent text to fortify his understanding of the new age that Jesus inaugurates by citing Jeremiah 31:31–34. Along with Isaiah's prediction that a messiah will be born among us who will be a wonderful counselor and a prince of peace (in Isaiah 9 and 11), no other text is more moving or filled with more hope for people of faith. The words speak to listeners of old, and to those of us lost in the violence of the twenty-first century, about the gentleness of God ("took them by the hand") and the divine determination to bring believers home and give them new life, even if a spiritual heart transplant is necessary.

A key concept in Jeremiah's testimony is obviously that of the central idea of *covenant*. In order to understand it completely, it is necessary for modern readers to turn to a Bible dictionary and a modern commentary on Jeremiah, but a few fundamental comments will be helpful here. One can see how important it is simply by noting that it appears in the NRSV translation of Hebrews some nineteen times, a dozen in the rest of the New Testament, and more than three hundred times in the Old Testament. Basically, the word *covenant* refers to a contract or an agreement between two parties that spells out mutually agreed obligations. It can be between a husband and wife, two friends, two states or nations, or, as is usually the case in the Old Testament, between God and the people of God.

In the Old Testament, covenant refers to God's promise to prevent further catastrophic floods (Gen. 6:18; 9:9, 11), the calling to Abraham to be the father of the nations (Gen. 12:1–3; 17:2), and the giving of the Ten Commandments and the law to Moses (Exod. 20:4–17; Deut. 5:1–21). By the time of King Josiah, Jews realized that the rejection of the covenant relationship with God through the sinful worship of idols already called for a new understanding of the law, and Jeremiah moved even further to call for an entirely new contract, one that is kept not by outward ritual but by inner spiritual commitment (see 2 Cor. 3:3). In the New Testament, Christians understood that this new relationship to God was to be derived only from belief in Jesus Christ, by following him and giving one's life to the One who died and was raised. In Hebrews the author sums up the importance of this new contract with God in 8:13 when he assures them that spiritual change is in the mind of God and in the heart of those who truly believe. The old covenant that demanded absolute obedience to the Hebrew law and required animal sacrifice is no longer operative. It is *obsolete*, it is *negans, nada*, antiquated, out of date, old. God will make all things new (Isa. 43:19; Rev. 21:5). Do you not see it?

? Questions for Reflection

1. How would you summarize the *main point* of Hebrews 8:1 in your own words?
2. How would this message about the possibility of a new relationship with God be good news to people you know?
3. Are there aspects of American religious life that need to be radically overhauled, that need a new temple, a new spiritual leader, a new high priest?
4. What is your relationship to God? What kind of a contract do you have with God? What happens if you break the agreement you think you have?

Jesus Christ Provides the Better Covenant and the Better Promises

Repetition and Expansion

In these verses the author of Hebrews repeats some of the concepts previously introduced in chapters 7 and 8 and moves on to expand his understanding of Jesus' relationship to the Old Testament covenant.

In the first part, for example, a contrast is drawn between worship under Judaism and what is foreseen in the new order of Christ. The description of Old Testament sacrifice and the arrangement of the tent of meeting is based somewhat loosely on Exodus 25–31 and selected passages from Leviticus and Numbers. Although he says in Hebrews 9:5 that he cannot speak about these things in much detail, he lingers on them throughout the whole chapter. It is helpful to define some key words so his purpose can be understood.

הֲקָמַת הַמִּשְׁכָּן עַל יְדֵי בְּנֵי יִשְׂרָאֵל בַּמִּדְבָּר

THE ERECTION OF THE TABERNACLE BY THE CHILDREN OF ISRAEL IN THE WILDERNESS

The Erection of the Tabernacle by the Children of Israel in the Wilderness (engraving) (B&W photo) by English School (19th century)

Holy of Holies The inner sanctum of the tent of meeting and later the Temple in Jerusalem where the ark of the covenant was kept (Exod. 28:29, 35, 43; Lev. 14:13; 16:1–27). Only the high priest could enter there once a year for the offering of atonement.

Lampstand   The seven branched candelabra made of pure gold found in the area outside the Holy of Holies. (See Exod. 25:31–40; 37:17–24; Lev. 24:4; Num. 8:2; Rev. 1:12–13, 20).

Bread of Presence   Twelve loaves placed on a table outside the Holy of Holies for a daily offering to the Lord. The priests were able to eat them as part of their holy portion. (See Lev. 24:5–9.)

Golden Altar of Incense   The place where the high priest (later other priests) burned perfumes made of aromatic ingredients to provide a pleasing odor to the Lord and avoid God's wrath (Exod. 40:26; Lev. 16:12–13; Num. 16:46–48).

Aaron's Rod   According to Numbers 17, Moses put the staff of Aaron and other tribal leaders in the tent of meeting to demonstrate their authority. When Aaron's sprouted leaves, it was God's way of showing that ultimate priestly power would come from his line.

Tablets   The two stones on which the Ten Commandments were written (Exod. 31:18; 34:1; Deut. 9:10; 2 Cor. 3:3).

Mercy Seat   The gold cover on top of the ark where the Commandments were kept in the Holy of Holies. It was believed that it was there that God's presence could be found (Lev. 16:2; Exod. 25:17–22).

Peter Paul Rubens, Flemish, 1577–1640
The Sacrifice of the Old Covenant (detail), about 1626

Cherubim of Glory   Messengers or angels from God (Gen. 3:24; Exod. 25:18–22; 26:1; 37:7–9; 2 Sam. 22:11; Isa. 37:16; Ezek. 9:3; 10:2–3; 28:14). On the ark of the covenant, images of two of them were made of hammered gold and placed at each end of the mercy seat, presumably functioning as sacred warnings.

Priestly Duties and Jesus' Continuing Ministry as High Priest

Hebrews 9:6–14 contrasts the functions of the priests of the tent of meeting with the activities of Jesus as the high priest in the new age to come. The lectures, the four final sections in chapter 9 (9:6–10, 11–14, 15–21, and 23–28) are designed to provide summaries of the main points that are being made.

> 9:9–10 The activities of the priests are symbols of the present time and indicate the imperfection of the old worship.
>
> 9:14 Christ offered himself to purify our conscience from dead works to worship the living God.
>
> 9:22 Without the shedding of blood there is no forgiveness of sin.
>
> 9:28 Christ, having been offered once, will appear a second time.

Verses 6–10 describe the ritual activities of the priests in the outer area of the tabernacle or the Temple, which probably included such service as the lighting of the lamps (Exod. 27:20), the offering of the bread (Exod. 25:30), and preparation of the incense (Exod. 30:8). To this is contrasted the duties of the high priest already mentioned in Hebrews 2:17; 3:1; 4:14f.; 6:20; 7:26–28; 8:1, 3, the one who only goes into the inner area, that is, the *second tent*, on the Day of Atonement. For *the blood that he offers for himself* see comments below on 7:27 (pp. 32–33). *Unintentionally* in 9:7 may indicate sin that the people commit without being aware of it. See the discussion above about 6:4–6 (p. 36).

What is meant by the expression *as long as the first tent is still standing* (9:8) is uncertain. It may signify the fact that no one goes into the Holy of Holies as long as rituals are performed in the outer court, but when the high priest enters the second tent, the way into it is opened. It could also be hinting at the fact that if the Temple of Herod has already been destroyed, there is no way into the Holy of Holies because it no longer exists. If this is the case, then it is all the more imperative that Jesus be seen as the true priest who really brings us into the presence of God. In any event, as v. 9 indicates, what goes on in the old tent is obsolete and old (8:13) because it cannot mature a worshiper spiritually (*cannot perfect the conscience of the worshiper*, 9:9) since the rituals there are mere observances of rules about the proper foods to eat, ritual cleansing (*various baptisms*), and purity rules.

The detailed priestly regulations about the proper animals that could be sacrificed at certain times, the different kinds of offerings that could be made, and definitions of bodily impurities that prevent true worship are outlined in Leviticus 1–15. The Gospel writers indicate that many of them still existed in Jesus' day and give his negative assessment of their value (Mark 1:21–28; 40–45; 2:18–22, 3:1–6; 7:1–23; and parallel passages in Matthew and Luke). In Hebrews objection to these rituals is not that Jesus himself rejected them but that they are ineffectual in and of themselves and are perfected only through the unblemished sacrifice of Jesus (9:14). The words *how much more* are central. If ancient rites of sacrifice were somewhat effective for cleansing the human body (*flesh*, 9:13), *how much more* will the death of Jesus deliver believers from reliance on keeping the law and lead them into the presence of the living God through the true forgiveness of sin?

New Covenant, New Metaphor (9:15–22)

Verses 15–22 introduce a new example which can be used to explain the difference between the law and the covenant of the new testament. Building on the efficacy of Jesus' death to bring redemption, the author points out that a will (another word for testament) is not effective until the person who made it is dead. The point of a will, as Paul points out in Galatians 3:15–18 (what he calls "an example from daily life"), is to make sure that no one can change it after the one who made it dies. Although it is difficult to follow the reasoning here in Hebrews, the point is made that the will of the Old Testament is also certified by death (the sacrifice of animals). Since this is the only way a will can be fulfilled, how much more valid is the will ratified through the blood shed by Jesus?

 Want To Know More?

About wills and testaments in the ancient world? See Craig R. Koester, *Hebrews: A New Translation*, Anchor Bible (New York: Doubleday, 2001), 418, 424–26. Clearly, this concept of the shedding of blood is a central image in both testaments. At the time Hebrews was written, it would be impossible to live in any major city of the world without being exposed to the sights of temples everywhere. No one could avoid the smell of burning flesh wafting through the streets and the sounds of dying animals and prayers and hymns being raised to the gods. As 1 Peter 1:18–19 puts it, "You know that you were ransomed from the futile ways inherited from your ancestors, not with perishable things like silver or gold, but with the precious blood of Christ, like that of a lamb without defect or blemish." The question that must be raised today, of course, is just how effective is this concept for an understanding of the atonement in the modern world? Since the concept of animal sacrifice is meaningless to us, how do we understand the efficacy of Jesus' death on the cross? Perhaps Paul's images in Romans 5:6–11 of someone giving a life for a friend or a person being willing to die even for an enemy are more meaningful. Possibly, the sacrifice that a mother would make by giving a kidney to her daughter or a soldier throwing himself on a grenade to save a fellow platoon member give us a clearer idea of what our early Christian forebears really meant.

The Temple as Symbol (9:23–28)

Chapter 9 is concluded with a return to the concept of the tent of meeting or the Jerusalem Temple as an ideal symbol of the differences between the old and new covenants. Luke Timothy Johnson points out that the contrast here between an earthly and a heavenly sanctuary fits within contemporary Jewish thought, especially as it is found in Jeremiah (7:1–15), Ezekiel 8–11, the apocryphal book called 2 Enoch, and in some writings from the Dead Sea community (L. T. Johnson, *Hebrews,* Excursus 6: Sanctuaries Material and Ideal, 227–32). As he summarizes this line of thought, the ideas in Hebrews fit "comfortably within a multifaceted spirit of longing within Judaism for a presence of God more powerful than that mediated by the cult of animal sacrifice. What distinguishes Hebrews in this, as in its language about covenant, is the author's conviction that this presence has been realized in the death and exaltation of Jesus" (Johnson, 232).

In Hebrews 9, the double appearance of the expression *again and again* in vv. 25 and 26 is a key one. If forgiveness of sin and redemption from God's punishment really are brought about by the shedding of blood, then it was necessary for the priests to practice it daily, day after day, and the high priest on the Day of Atonement to offer up annual sacrifices, *year after year* (10:1, 3). In Jesus' death, however, we see a sacrifice that does not have to be offered over and over again since he has appeared *once for all* to bear the sins of many.

Reprise (10:1–18)

In 10:1 (and in 9:23), Hebrews accents the imagery from Platonic thought that appeared earlier in 8:5 that shows how the old covenant is only a *shadow* or a *sketch* of spiritual reality. Similarly, this section returns to the idea that Jesus himself and the Holy Spirit are both speaking through Old Testament texts (see comments above, pp. 12, 19), in this case Psalm 40:6–8; Jeremiah 36; and the important texts already used extensively in earlier chapters, that is, Psalm 110 and Jeremiah 31:31–34. These texts clinch the argument started in Hebrews 7:7, repeated in 8:13, and finalized here. Since the perfect sacrifice has been made in Jesus, as 10:18 puts it, there is no longer any need for the offering of sin at any time or in any place, ever again.

? Questions for Reflection

1. If you were trying to explain the significance of Jesus' birth to a non-Christian, what modern illustrations would you use it to make it clearer?
2. The reference to the blood of Jesus is a key component of the celebration of the Lord's Supper. What do the words "This is my blood shed for you" signify?
3. What does it mean that Jesus died "once for all"?
4. Do you agree that "without the shedding of blood there is no forgiveness of sins"? (9:22)

8 Hebrews 10:19–11:40

The Practical Consequences of His Superiority

Six Key Verses

As Hebrews moves inexorably toward its final chapters, this eighth section provides one of most encouraging and hope-filled homilies in the whole New Testament. The keys to its positive assessment of the Christian faith are found in six central texts.

> 10:19–20 We have confidence in Jesus through a new and living way.
>
> 10:24 Our faith allows us to provoke one another to love.
>
> 10:32 We do not shrink back from a hard struggle with sufferings.
>
> 11:1 Faith is the assurance of things hoped for and the conviction of things not seen.
>
> 11:13 Heroes of faith in the past provide us with powerful examples; they saw the promises of God from a distance, but they believed without receiving them.
>
> 11:39–40 God provides something even better than promises, through Jesus Christ.

A New and Living Way (10:19–22)

In vv. 19–22 the author returns to a subject of importance to him, Jesus' relationship to the tent of meeting and the way we are led into God's presence through him. Moving from the earlier example (Jesus is not only *like* the covenant; he *is* the covenant), here he argues that Jesus does more than provide an entrance to the area of sacrifice; he himself is the entryway (Greek: *eisodos)* to the worship area. He not only is the true high priest who goes through the curtain (Greek: *katapetasma*) separating the vestibule to the Temple and the Holy of Holies, but he *becomes* that curtain.

The image used here of the entryway is one that would have been familiar to all his readers, Jewish and Gentile, because in temples around the world it was the access point (cf. 2 Pet. 1:11) to sacred spaces. His description is so graphic that it is almost like a digitized virtual tour that helps his readers imagine how Jesus provides the way to God, that is, through the sacrifice of his flesh on the cross. The curtain, of course, is the one described in Exodus 26:36–37; 38:18 and other Old Testament texts—the one that is ripped in half on Good Friday when Jesus dies (Matt. 27:51; Mark 15:38). It becomes a primary symbol of hope and encouragement, since Jesus not only enters into the presence of God through it but personifies that presence for all who believe in him. Because of Jesus' symbolic and actual entrance into God's house, believers can now approach God with the *full assurance of faith* mentioned in Hebrews 10:21 (Greek, *plerophoria*; cf. Col. 2:2; 1 Thess. 1:5; Heb. 6:11) and hold on to their confession of hope without wavering.

For definitions of *house* (Heb. 10:21) and *confession* (v. 23), see Unit 4 above (pp. 26–27). The *Day* in v. 25 is a reference to the expected return of Christ when he will bring judgment to individuals and to the nations, when history will be wrapped up and God's purposes will finally be made clear. (See 1 Thess. 5:2, 4; 2 Thess. 1:10; 2:2–3; 2 Tim. 1:12, 18; 4:8; 2 Pet. 3:10, 12; Jude 6). A similar concept is implied in the quotation of Habakkuk 2:3 in Hebrews 10:37 below, "one who is coming will come and will not delay."

The use of the word *way* in "the new and living way" in verse 20 also provides another graphic image through which readers may visualize what Jesus does for them. It is like an animation or a video presentation that allows the believer to retrace the whole concept of Exodus. The way is the path God provides through the Red Sea as the people escape the Egyptian army. It is the long, torturous route through the Sinai for forty years in which they are led both day and night. The way of God is also the one imagined by Old Testament prophets (Mark 1:2; see Isa. 40:3; Mal. 3:1) and introduced by John the Baptist as God prepares for God's coming in Jesus Christ. The way is the road that Jesus takes later on, one of discipleship (Mark 8:27; 9:33–34) and suffering (Mark 10:52) that leads directly to Jerusalem. In the early church it truly does become a "living way," as the Christian movement is defined as the pilgrimage of faith spelled with a capital W, the Way of God (Acts 9:2; 19:23; 22:4; 24:22; 25:3), the way of truth (2 Pet. 2:2).

Provoke One Another to Love (10:24–25)

The manner in which the church makes its journey alive and vital is summarized in Hebrews 10:24–25: by provoking one another to love and maintaining regular worship and fellowship. The Greek word "provoke" (*paroxusmos*) in verse 24 is a strong, almost violent one and is the root of the English word "paroxysm," which can refer to a powerful outpouring of emotion or a sudden or ongoing attack of a disease (like a high fever) that can cause one to shudder or have the shakes. Clearly, "to provoke" can have a negative overtone or indicate an action that drives someone to anger (cf. Jer. 44:8; Acts 17:16). But in Hebrews 10, where it is closely connected with positive images of hope, it has the sense of encouraging or stimulating someone to respond with concern and charity to others. In Xenophon's *Memorabilia* (III), for example, a man complains about the terrible relationship he has with his brother. After asking some leading questions about the way he responds to his brother's snarling nature, Socrates finally advises him to change his attitude and endeavor to provoke or tame him by kindness. Somewhat similarly, Plutarch describes Cimon as a statesman who dealt gently with others and was able to "incite" them to right behavior (*Cimon* 16.3). Perhaps what is in mind here in Hebrews is a positive way of saying what Paul points out in 1 Corinthians 13:4–7, that love is not irritable or resentful; it is patient and kind. It bears, believes, hopes, and endures. As Hebrews 10:25 indicates, true Christian love leads to regular fellowship and mutual encouragement.

The Situation the Readers Face (10:32–39)

Skipping over 10:26–31 (see the discussion of apostasy above, in Unit 4, p. 30 and Unit 5, p. 36), it is evident that the next section (10: 32–39), about the abuse and the persecution suffered by the recipients of Hebrews, provides central insights into the reasons why the sermon was written in the first place. As the introduction points out (pp. 4–5), scholars are not certain about the exact date of the composition of Hebrews. Some of the description of the readers' terrible experiences in 10:32–39 is parallel to that which was predicted by Jesus (see Mark 13 and the parallels), the imprisonments endured by the first apostles (see Acts), and the humiliations, beatings, "insults, hardships, persecutions, and calamities" that Paul endured before his trial in Rome (see Acts 21–28; 2 Cor. 12:10; and see a longer list in 2 Cor. 11:16–12:9) prior to 70 CE. A close examination of Hebrews 10:32 ff., however, and the description of readers' being exposed to public ridicule and having to abandon their homes are reminiscent of the situations described in books like 1 and 2 Peter, Jude, and Revelation, which were written at the end of the first century. Hebrews 10:32–39 provides an introduction to the long list of the heroes and heroines of faith in chapter 11, which by its very length demonstrates that the situation is so severe, possibly even involving official Roman persecution and military terrorism, that the author feels compelled to provide numerous examples and words of encouragement to keep his readers from shrinking back (10:39). In 1 Peter, for example, Christians are in a similar difficult situation, having their faith tried by fire (1:6–7; 4:12). They are being called "aliens and exiles" (2:11; see Heb. 11:13, "strangers and foreigners"), murderers, thieves, criminals, and mischief makers (1 Pet. 4:15). Similarly, in 2 Peter in a list reminiscent of Hebrews 11 (see the discussion below), a comparison is made between the sufferings the readers are enduring and those of angels, Noah, and Lot, and the author encourages them to have faith under trial (2 Pet. 2:4–10). In Jude, furthermore, possibly the last book of the New Testament to be written, it is said that the readers who are viciously slandered by opponents (Jude 10) must be encouraged to stand fast in Jesus Christ, "who is able to keep you from falling" (v. 24). The similarity of these situations, therefore, and the style of writing in Hebrews, which resembles that found in these books in many ways, suggest that Hebrews may also have been written after 90 CE, when the church sustained long periods of persecution in many regions of the Roman Empire.

The Conviction of Things Not Seen (11:1–3)

The central definition of faith in Hebrews 11:1–3, one that probably provides the best-known quotation from Hebrews to modern readers ("Now faith is the assurance of things hoped for, the conviction of things not seen"), is introduced in 10:37–38, "my righteous one shall live by faith," by reinterpreting Habakkuk 2:4. When Paul uses this same Old Testament prophecy in Romans 1:17 and Galatians 3:11, he cites it to distance himself from a Jewish system of forgiveness which he considers to be outmoded, that is, the idea of salvation through works. Here, however, the author of Hebrews paraphrases the text from Habakkuk to encourage his readers and hearers to have faith in promises that are invisible, ones that have not been completely fulfilled.

It is not difficult to see how the call to *conviction of things not seen* could be a word of real comfort, especially at a time when the people of faith were in turmoil and danger. But how does this fly in an age that relies primarily on visual and audio cues to learn and believe? In the churches of the twenty-first century, communication is being made possible more and more through computerized presentations projected on large screens during worship. We carry our wireless phones in our pockets, and they not only allow us to hear each other but miniaturized screens provide news and entertainment from anywhere in the world. We travel in the digitized cocoons of our own making, woven through electronic webs by our iPods, MP3 players, and Bluetooth devices. We very much believe in things we can see and hear.

Yet, like the author of Hebrews, we know that the most important things in life cannot always be measured, quantified, and recorded. He sees God at work in the lives of believers through very concrete events, through acts of faithfulness, sacrifice, love, and belief in the promises of God. Today we see God at work similarly in the love a mother has for her child or in the sacrifice a father makes when he is willing to give a kidney for his daughter. We see the example of Christ being displayed when a man jumps in front on an onrushing subway train to rescue a stranger without thinking about the risk to his own life. We know that God is at work in missionaries who dedicate their whole lives to bring healing and justice to brothers and sisters all over the world. In every

---

Want to Know More?

About Abel and Cain? See Genesis chap. 4; Matthew 23:35; Luke 11:51; Hebrews 12:24; 1 John 3:12; Jude 11. Why was Abel's sacrifice considered better than Cain's?

About Enoch? See Genesis 4:17–18; 5:18–24; 1 Chronicles 1:3; Luke 3:37; Jude 14. He is described as one who walked with God. Note that the apocryphal books of 1 and 2 Enoch (written during a long period from perhaps 300 BCE to 300 CE) purport to tell about his heavenly visions.

About Noah? See Genesis 5:29–10:32; Isaiah 54:9; Ezekiel 14:14, 20; Luke 3:36; 17:26–27; 1 Peter 3:20; 2 Peter 2:5.

About Abraham? See the discussion in Unit 5 above and Hebrews 2:16; 6:13–15; 7:1–9; Genesis 11:27–25:11; Romans 4:1–16; 9:7; 11:1; Galatians 3:6–5:1; James 2:21–23; 1 Peter 3:6.

About Sarah? See Genesis 17:15–25:10; 49:31; Isaiah 51:2; Romans 9:9; 1 Peter 3:6. Note that she is one of two women included in this list of heroes of faith. The other one is **Rahab**, a prostitute who helped the Israelites spy on Jericho, Joshua 2:1–7; 6:17, 23–25. Note how she is listed among the ancestors of Jesus in Matthew's genealogy, the grandmother of Ruth's husband, Matthew 1:5. Also see James 2:25, where it is said that she was justified by her works.

About Isaac? See Genesis 22:1–19 and his near sacrifice to God; his blessing of his son **Jacob** instead of the elder son, **Esau**, Genesis 27:1–40. Note that tradition says that Abraham offered him to God on the site where the Holy of Holies was constructed in the Jerusalem Temple.

About Moses? See the discussion above, in Unit 4.

For detailed information see Luke Timothy Johnson, *Hebrews, A Commentary*, 274–312. For a shorter, more concise list, see Leonard T. Wolcott, *Hebrews* (Nashville: Abingdon Press, 1988), 108–25.

century there are intangible aspects of faith that must be felt to be believed. But we also learn through example, by the words and actions of those who have gone before us who show us how faith and action really go together.

The Heroes of Faith (11:4–40)

Hebrews 11 is a wonderful chapter, which provides information about fifteen heroes and heroines of faith that are listed by name. It is virtually a "Who's Who" of Jewish exemplars and mentors, along with the prophets mentioned in verses 32–33 and all those hinted at in verses 34–38. The box on the previous page provides some scriptural references about a few of them in order to enable us to see why they are placed in Hebrews' spiritual hall of fame. For detailed information, it will be necessary to consult other commentaries or Bible dictionaries.

 ## Questions for Reflection

1. If you were to make a list of the people who have influenced your faith, whose names would be on it?
2. Who are the believers mentioned in 11:32–38? Take a look at 1 and 2 Maccabees in the Apocrypha and read about the terrible suffering the Jews experienced during the Maccabean revolt from about 167 to 137 BCE. Read about the attempted genocide in 3 Maccabees and the celebration of the martyrs in 4 Maccabees. Can you see how they may be in mind in this chapter of Hebrews?
3. Do you think that faith without sight is comforting to people who have suffered excruciating persecution for their beliefs? What about the victims of the Holocaust? What about Christian missionaries who were murdered in places like El Salvador or Pakistan? How does your faith help you when you suffer?
4. Can you think of any time when someone attempted to provoke you to love? Does this have anything to do with "tough love"?

9 Hebrews 12:1–13:17

Concluding Advice: Continue to Run the Race with Total Determination

As the last full section of Hebrews is brought to a close, its author continues with a familiar form of argument to provide some practical advice. Using additional Old Testament examples—Esau (12:15–17), Moses (12:18–21), and Abel (12:24)—select scripture quotations (Heb. 12:5–6; 12:20–21; 12:26–27; 13:6), and some more concepts drawn from Platonic philosophy (12:18–21), concrete suggestions are offered about keeping faith strong through practice and discipline. Some of the vocabulary is unique and appears nowhere else in the New Testament. Greek words translated as "cloud," "weight" (12:1), "pioneer," "perfecter" (12:2), "struggle" (12:4), "illegitimate" (12:8), "reverence," "awe" (12:28), and "helper" (13:6) indicate the independence of the author's thought and his desire to enable his readers to think about Christian faith and action in new ways.

This last major section of the book also draws on imaginative images and metaphors that make immediate sense to readers living in the twenty-first century, such as the church as a living organism, the analogy of preparing for an athletic event, references to education and family life, encouragement to believers who live in a shaky world that seems to be falling apart, and the positive value of love and respect.

The Church as Ongoing Organism

The author begins chapter 12 with a reference to the church as an organic entity, one that has a past, present, and future through the people who were, are, or will be members of it. On certain occasions when a congregation celebrates the Lord's Supper, especially on World Communion or a Sunday near All Saints' Day, it may occur to us what he means in 12:1 when he writes that we are surrounded by a great "cloud of witnesses." There it refers back to chapter 11 and the heroes and heroines of faith who laid the foundation for the present readers. "Cloud" could also indicate the heavenly host that surrounds God's throne (cf. Ps. 148:2; Isa. 6:1–3; Luke 2:13; Rev. 4:1–9), or even the angels mentioned in Hebrews 1 and 2. In our case, we can be reminded of the believers who preceded us as members, elders, deacons, or pastors, many of whom may have passed away years ago, people who stood around one Communion table and witnessed to Jesus Christ in their own time and place so that we might continue as a congregation. These are the saints who from their labors rest. They are part of a blest communion that enables us to do God's work now in spite of the struggles we must face. Now we serve the same function for those who will come in the next generations. They will stand on our shoulders as they minister in Christ's name in situations we cannot imagine.

For the author of Hebrews, Jesus also serves as a major witness in this developing history. Building on an image used previously of Jesus as the *pioneer* (see 2:10 and Unit 3 above), he is also described in 12:2 at the other end of the spectrum as the *perfecter of our faith*. "Perfecter" is taken from Greek roots (*teleō, teleioō*) that refer to a process of completion, bringing something to an end, leading to full maturity. Similar vocabulary is used elsewhere in the New Testament to describe the carrying out of scriptural prophecies (Acts 13:29) and the fulfillment of the royal law of love (Jas. 2:8). In Hebrews Jesus is said to be made *perfect* through sufferings (2:10; 5:9), *perfect forever* (7:28). By his sacrifice he has made all those complete who believe in him (10:14; 11:40). The idea is that Jesus is guiding God's process throughout all of history and providing continuity to the faithful in the past, present, and future; "Jesus Christ is the same yesterday and today and forever" (13:8). The same promise is attributed to Jesus himself in Rev. 22:13 where he says, "I am the Alpha and the Omega, the first and the last, the beginning and the end."

Jesus as the Model in the Faith Race (12:1–3)

The sports model for Christian faith that is suggested in the words "let us run with perseverance the race that is set before us" is a second image that is very meaningful to readers today. Chapter 12:11 returns to the same theme with the word *trained* (Greek: *gegymnasmenois*) as it pictures young men working out in a Greco-Roman gymnasium. In a world that has a major interest in sporting events that serve to entertain us, foster national pride, and build incentive and character for millions of children and young people, we can easily understand how athletic events can serve as helpful metaphors for Christian endurance. The original readers would have been familiar with the great competitions held in Athens, Sparta, Olympia, Corinth, Rome, in the city of Caesarea in Israel, and throughout the whole Roman Empire. Through contests in track and field, drama, poetry, and music, citizens trained vigorously to win the first prize of a wreath of olive or laurel leaves for their heads, and the recognition that went with it. As Paul puts it in 1 Corinthians 9:24ff.: "Do you not know that in a race the runners all compete, but only one receives the prize? Run in such a way that you may win it. Athletes exercise self-control in all things; they do it to receive a perishable wreath, but we an imperishable one." Or as the author of 2 Timothy 4:7–8 writes, "I have fought the good fight, I have finished the race, I have kept the faith. From now on there is reserved for me the crown of righteousness." Other references to the games and the Christian life are found in Galatians 5:7; 1 Timothy 4:8; 2 Tim. 2:5; James 1:12; 1 Peter 5:4; and Revelation 2:10.

Want To Know More?

About ancient athletic contests? See Leslie Adkins and Roy A. Adkins, *Handbook to Life in Ancient Rome* (New York: Oxford University Press, 1994), 141–42; James S. Jeffers, *The Greco-Roman World of the New Testament Era* (Downers Grove, Ill.: InterVarsity Press, 1999), 31–34; Luke Timothy Johnson, *Hebrews: A Commentary*, New Testament Library (Louisville, Ky.: Westminster John Knox Press, 2006), 315–23.

In Hebrews 12, readers who are undergoing persecution and trials are encouraged to train hard and not give up the spiritual race they are in. They need the training and discipline that God offers (vv. 3–11); they must strengthen weakened knees and legs to run a straight line to the finish (vv. 12–13). The prime example of such perseverance is found in Jesus. Because he had to endure ridicule at the hands of his enemies ("endured . . . hostility against himself from sinners," v. 3), and had to suffer the shame of a public execution and punishment as a common criminal without abandoning the race God placed him in, they should remember his example and not run out of spiritual energy or get discouraged.

Examples from Education and Family Life

Additional metaphors for the rigors of the Christian life are developed in 12:3–17, with reference to the need for disciplined education and adherence to family traditions. Verses 3–11 are based on Proverbs 3:11–12 and the teachings found in Jewish Wisdom literature.

Using an image often found in the New Testament that compares church members to children, that is, children of God (see John 1:12; 12:36; 13:33; Rom. 8:14–16; Gal. 3:26; 4:28; 1 Thess. 5:5; 1 John 2:18; 3:1), the readers are urged to think of their trials as God's discipline rather than punishment. In the patriarchal society of the first century CE, it was commonly understood that men ran families and the entire household (see Eph. 5:21–6:4; Col. 3:18–21 for examples). If human fathers expected obedience from their children and provided them with benefits as heirs, how much more would God as a heavenly Father give to members of the family of faith? Although parents discipline us for only a short time until we grow up, God is part of our life forever, and God's purpose is "for our good, in order that we may share his holiness" (Heb 12:10). God's teaching is never oppressive or damaging, but always "peaceful" (v. 11).

Today, of course, believers are less likely than their first-century counterparts to attribute suffering to God, even if it leads to good. Such thoroughgoing determinism seems heartless to many people, and twenty-first century Christians pinpoint the scientific and human causes of tragedy rather than thinking that God creates them for the purpose of enforcing obedience.

> Wisdom literature refers to Proverbs, Job, Ecclesiastes in the Old Testament, and the Wisdom of Jesus Son of Sirach and the Wisdom of Solomon in the Apocrypha. Two of its characteristics are to teach about the fear of the Lord and to show how discipline, self-control, honesty, and common sense can lead believers on the right path. Some of Jesus' teachings in the Sermon on the Mount and the admonitions in James come from similar traditions. See "Wisdom Literature in the OT," *HarperCollins Bible Dictionary*.

For the writer of Hebrews, however, the case about discipline needs to be pushed even further. In his view, obedience proves that one is a true son or daughter of God. Those who do not accept God's discipline demonstrate that they are *illegitimate* (Greek *nothoi*, i.e., bastards) and have no rights in the family.

A prime example is found in the story of Esau. In Jewish literature, Esau illustrated the mistakes of a person who did not respect family tradition and claim his rightful inheritance as the oldest son and the true heir of his father's blessing (Gen. 27:18–40). Although nothing is said in the Genesis account about his moral deficiencies, the author of Hebrews calls him immoral (*pornos* in Greek), godless or profane (cf. 1 Tim. 1:9; 4:7). In the ancient world the eldest son, or the firstborn (*prōtotokos*), was the one who inherited all the father's property and wealth (compare the interpretation of the story of Abraham's sons, Isaac and Ishmael, in Galatians 4:21–5:1). For Greeks and Romans, furthermore, it was usually only the first son who was given the right to an education. For both Jews and Gentiles, therefore, it was inconceivable that anyone would allow himself to be tricked out of his birthright. To do so was a sign of infidelity to God, of covenant breaking.

> Parents subject the still malleable characters of their children to what will do them good. Let them cry and struggle as they will, we swaddle them tightly lest their still immature bodies become deformed rather than straight and tall. Later we instill liberal culture by means of terror if they refuse to learn. (Seneca, *Moral Epistles* 47, cited by Jeffers, 237)

Cain's improper offering and his murder of his brother Abel provides a second example (Heb. 12:24). As Hebrews 12:23 points out in an unusual expression, only those who are of *the assembly of the firstborn* (Greeks, *ecclēsia prōtotokōn*) can be enrolled in heaven. Although Esau was restored to his brother in the Genesis account (Gen. 33:1–15), the judgment in Hebrews is much harsher, and he is seen as an illustration of the danger of apostasy (see the discussion above in Units 4 and 5), a sin so great that one could not repent for it (Heb. 12:17). Cain, on the other hand, was cast out of God's presence and was forced to live east of Eden, where he could never see his family again.

In the modern church, even though we understand the point that is being made about education and discipline, we are likely to reinterpret it for readers today. For us, education is not so much a matter of strict requirements of behavior and the maintenance of formal family norms as it is an opportunity to learn new things, build character, and find ways to make a better life. In our Christian faith, the journey through life can be seen as one in which we are constantly learning about God, perpetually making discoveries about human nature, the wonders of the earth, and God's creative process. To make the most of this, to benefit from a high school education, to finish college, or to make one's way through a master's or Ph.D. program, students must be extremely disciplined and must be willing to invest large amounts of time and money to achieve a desired reward that could last an entire lifetime. For us, discipline in faith has to do more with the effort we are willing to put in, rather than the way God pushes us to obey. As it is stated in 1 Timothy 4:7–8, "Train yourself in godliness, for, while physical training is of some value, godliness is valuable in every way, holding promise for both the present life and the life to come."

The final section of chapter 12, verses 18–28, somewhat abruptly shifts focus from education and family to a pyrotechnic account of Moses' experience on Mount Sinai, the terrifying and bone-rattling experience of meeting God, and the danger readers live in as the whole world seems to be crashing down around them. Based on the accounts of the giving of the Ten Commandments in Exodus 19–20 and Deuteronomy 4–5, the author reminds them of the frightening aspects of encountering God when the mountain shook and God spoke through thunder (Exod. 19:16–19). The power of God was so awesome that the people could not even approach or talk to God (19:12–13, 21). Now, however, he wants them to know that they can anticipate a wonderful new relationship with God through Jesus Christ, one in which they will find the true Mount Zion (the place on which the Temple was built) and *the heavenly Jerusalem*. As Luke Timothy Johnson points out, this Old Testament imagery is linked with the Platonic worldview that the material world one sees is always inferior to the world that is not seen, the one that is heavenly and eternal (*Hebrews*, 330–35). The new city of Jerusalem in Hebrews is similar to the one described in Revelation 21:1–7, a place where all suffering and tears will be removed and believers will truly be God's children. This promise of a new heavenly dwelling place gives hope and courage for the future. As it is summarized in Hebrews 13:14, "For here we have no lasting city, but we are looking for the city that is to come."

Quoting from Haggai 2:6 in Hebrews 12:26, the author continues to promise his readers that the suffering and trials they are currently experiencing do not represent ultimate reality. God is like the consuming fire seen by Moses in the burning bush (Exod. 3:1–6), like the dangerous divine presence on Mount Sinai, the one that will separate appearances from truth (Exod. 24:17; Deut. 4:24). When believers understand the power and purposes of God they can respond with respect, worship, and true piety (Heb. 12:28). And so in all times and all places, whenever Christians find themselves threatened with terrorism, war, and violence at home and abroad, and they worry that the world is disintegrating, Hebrews reminds them to pay attention to the eternal plan of God that through Christ they will receive *a kingdom that cannot be shaken*. As Psalm 46 puts it, "God is our refuge and strength, a very present help in trouble. Therefore we will not fear, though the earth should change, though the mountains should shake in the heart of the sea."

Always Extend Love
and Show Commitment (13:1–17)

In the first verses of the last chapter, additional practical advice is given about several unrelated issues that are loosely strung together like beads on a necklace.

In Hebrews 13:1, for example, the encouragement for readers to regard each other in *mutual love* is a general admonition that is reminiscent of the teaching in 10:24 (see Unit 8, pp. 50–51 above). In Greek, the word used for love here (*philadelphia*) can be literally translated "brotherly love" and reminds us of the great love chapters elsewhere in the New Testament, like those found in 1 Corinthians 13 or 1 John 4 (also see Rom. 12:10; 1 Pet. 1:22; 3:8). That mutual love for a wide range of people was a normal expectation in the Greco-Roman world is indicated by Paul's acknowledgment that the readers of Thessalonians loved all the brothers and sisters throughout Macedonia (1 Thess. 4:9–12), and also by a whole city given the name Philadelphia (Rev. 3:7).

Hebrews 13:2 continues with the same idea by encouraging the extension of hospitality to all people. Hospitality was very important in an age when travelers had to depend on the goodwill of people along the way in order to move from place to place in the Roman Empire. In Greek (*philoxenias*), it literally means "love of stranger," and is listed as one of the genuine results of spiritual love in Romans 12:13 (also see 1 Pet. 4:9). The idea of entertaining angels without knowing it is probably derived from the story of Abraham and Lot and their encounter with angels in Genesis 18–19.

The admonition to remember prisoners in Hebrews 13:3 no doubt reflects experiences of some of the readers or their friends and relatives as they faced official persecution for their beliefs. Since some of them had been incarcerated themselves, they should care about those who were undergoing similar mistreatment (cf. 10:34). Verses 4 and 5 represent the general kind of advice that is given about principles of sharing and stewardship (see 1 Cor. 9, Jas. 2:14–17, for examples), the sanctity of marriage required by the Ten Commandments (Exod. 20:14), and avoidance of sexual immorality (Matt. 5:27–32). The warning about *love of money* is reminiscent of 1 Timothy 6:10 (see 2 Tim. 3:2) and Jesus' teaching about the danger of possessions (see Luke 16:14; Matt. 6:19–21, 25–34).

In Hebrews 13:7 and 17 directions are given about the support of church leaders, who preach the word of God. Since this is the chief way in which God communicates to believers, that is, through the speech and examples provided by those whom are sent (see 1:1), it is important that they be shown proper respect. Apparently, some people had rejected what they had been taught and had chased after mythological speculations and strange teachings, possibly various theories about Jesus' true relationship to God. What is more, some had also been influenced by Jewish regulations about food, probably like those found in parts of the Old Testament. The author bluntly says that they are of no benefit whatsoever.

Finally, Hebrews returns to the important conviction that the way sacrifice for sin is usually conducted is outmoded and dangerous. Jesus is the high priest who offers himself as the ultimate blood sacrifice to God. "Outside the city" in verse 12 refers to the fact that things that were considered unorthodox or forbidden were taken outside the boundaries of the city to be destroyed (Exod. 29:14; Lev. 4:11–12; 9:11; 16:27). Since Jesus was crucified beyond the walls of Jerusalem (Matt. 27:31; Luke 23:32) on Golgotha, according to Jewish and Roman law about the execution of a criminal (Lev. 24:14, 23; Num. 15:35–36; Acts 7:58), his death shows that God is drawing new boundaries about what is in or out, what is clean and what is unclean. The author of Hebrews wants readers to leave the security of so-called holy or clean places in the Temple or the tent of meeting to offer the true sacrifices that are pleasing to God, that is, the confession of Jesus as Son of God, and the offering of lives that are generous and committed to doing good (Heb. 13:15–16; cf. Gal. 6:10; 3 John 11).

? Questions for Reflection

1. Who were the pioneers of your congregation? Do you know what problems and opportunities they faced? How can you thank God for their contributions?
2. How can athletics be used as a metaphor for the Christian faith today? In what ways is the extreme emphasis on sports in the twenty-first century inimical to what Hebrews was trying to teach?
3. Do you know anyone who has the special spiritual gift of hospitality? How is it shown in that one's life?
4. In what ways is love of money a serious spiritual danger in our society today? Do you see any ways in which it influences stewardship in your church?

Final Greetings and Summation

Hebrews concludes with closing requests, summary remarks, and a benediction asking for God's blessings that are typical of other letters in the New Testament and with formulas found in epistles in general in the first century. Many of the comments in Hebrews 13:18–19, for example, are found in other New Testament letters, such as the request for prayers for the author (see Eph. 6:18–19; 1 Thess. 5:25); the review of travel plans (Rom. 15:28–29; 1 Cor. 16:15–17; 2 Tim. 4:21; Titus 3:12–13; Phlm. 22); benedictions asking God for peace (Rom. 16:20; Phil. 4:9; Col. 4:5–6), and the like. Although it is clear that the readers of Hebrews were in a dangerous situation and really needed peace from God, these last verses do not provide any more information about their actual situation, since, unlike Paul's letters, there are no names listed of people in the church, no personal greetings are given, no specific issues are addressed, and no detailed projections about future contacts or communications are given. Thus, in spite of a somewhat conventional ending for letters, it remains clear that Hebrews is like a sermon or tract intended for a wide audience rather than a letter for a specific group of church members in one location. (See the discussion in the introduction, pp. 2–3).

> Dionysus to Nikanor his dearest friend, greetings. I request, brother, that you help my brother Demetrios, until he gets the grain measured. For I am still in a critical state, even now. And you know that you are not providing (help) to a person lacking in gratitude. I know your goodness. Farewell, dearest friend. And further, when I was with you I paid attention to your interests. (A papyrus letter from Oxyrhychos, G.H.R. Horsley, *New Documents Illustrating Christianity*, v.4 [Marrickville, Australia: Southwood Press, 1987], 56)

The author asks for the listeners' support, assuring them of his honorable conduct and good intentions. References to *a clear conscience* (literally, a *good* conscience in Greek) appear elsewhere in the New Testament with the implication that it is informed by the action of the Holy Spirit in the inner person. See Acts 23:1; 1 Peter 3:13–16, 21 for a connection between conduct and conscience and the warning in 1 Timothy 1:5, 19 about people who reject good conscience and make a shipwreck of their faith. Proper conduct has already been mentioned in Hebrews 13:7 as the mark of leaders.

Verses 20–21 contain a moving benediction that is still used at the close of services today. *The God of peace* points to the belief that God is the one who can stop violence and bring spiritual comfort (Num. 6:26; 25:12; Ps. 29:11; Isa. 26:12; Rom. 15:33; 16:20; Eph. 1:2; Phil. 4:9; 1 Thess. 5:23), and the Christian conviction that Jesus not only brings peace, but is our peace (Eph. 2:14). It is this same God who raised Jesus from the dead through the covenant that is a central feature of the theology of Hebrews. This is the first time in this book that Jesus is referred to as *the great shepherd of the sheep*, but the conclusion follows: since sacrifice is required to save believers from sin, and Jesus becomes the offering that is required, not only is he the lamb of God, but he is the one who cares for God's flock (cf. John 10:11, 14; 1 Pet. 2:25; 5:4; Rev. 7:17). Jesus says in Mark 6:34 that the people are like sheep

Christian sarcophagus (marble) by Roman (2rd century AD)

without a shepherd (see Num. 27:17; 1 Kings 22:17; 2 Chron. 18:16; Ezek. 34:5), and the implication is that God himself will become that shepherd through him. As it is promised in Ezekiel 34:11, 15, "For thus says the Lord GOD; I myself will search for my sheep, and will seek them out. . . . I myself will be the shepherd of my sheep, and I will make them lie down, says the Lord GOD." In later Christian art, especially in sarcophagi and in the catacombs, the image of Jesus carrying a lamb became a primary symbol of faith.

In Hebrews 13:22 the author asks the readers to *bear with my word of exhortation.* Possibly, he thinks that it is too long, even though he says that he has written *briefly*. Indeed, Hebrews is one of the longer "letters" in the New Testament, but to a congregation gathered to hear a sermon or an exposition of faith, a one-hour address would probably not seem excessive. *Exhortation* (*paraklēsis* in Greek) is the description he gives to his whole work. It means "encouragement, comfort, consolation," "teaching," or "warning," and refers to a style of formal rhetorical writing that offers advice (Acts 13:15;15:31; Phil. 2:1). See the discussion in Unit 3, p. 18.

In Hebrews 13:23 a reference is made to Timothy. This is the only personal name mentioned in the whole letter, and it is difficult to know how to assess its significance. Presumably, it is a reference to the travel companion of Paul, who served as his emissary and secretary. Paul went out of his way to permit him to be circumcised (Acts 16:1) and took him on his second missionary journey (Acts 16:1–4; 17:14–15; 18:5). Why he is mentioned in Hebrews is unclear. If he was still alive at the time of composition, it might help determine when it was written. Since the letters of 1 and 2 Timothy are generally understood not to have been written by him but by someone else who was using his name to lend more authority to the work, however, it is possible that his name is added in Hebrews 13:23 for a similar reason, perhaps even to connect the sermon with the work of Paul. In any case, the presence of his name here cannot be given much weight in the interpretation of Hebrews, especially since the author's identity remains unknown.

Want to Know More?

About exhortation and rhetoric? See Craig R. Koester, *Hebrews: A New Translation* Anchor Bible (New York: Doubleday, 80–82).

In the final comment in verse 24, it is said that *those from Italy send you greetings*. Once again, this reference is too general to know what it means. *Those from Italy* could be acquaintances of the author who live in the city of Rome or somewhere else in Italy. They also might be Christians living in a Roman colony anywhere in the Roman Empire. Acts 18:2 mentions the fact that Paul's backers, Aquila and his wife, Priscilla, had come *from Italy*, forced out by the persecutions of Emperor Claudius. Perhaps the reference here is a code that indicates a similar predicament that the readers of Hebrews face presently under the current administration in Rome.

The closing words of the sermon reflect common practice in most New Testament letters where a reference to God's great gift in Jesus Christ (*Grace be with all of you*) replaces the more common ending used in the Roman Empire: "Farewell" (see 2 Thess. 3:18;1 Tim. 6:21; 2 Tim. 4:22; Titus 3:15; Phlm. 25, for examples). It reminds believers of their special calling through Jesus Christ and the fact that he will help them no matter what might come next, "Let us therefore approach the throne of grace with boldness, so that we may receive mercy and find grace to help in time of need" (Heb. 4:16).

Conclusions

What can we say finally about the study of the book of Hebrews? It is possible to see how valuable it is for our understanding of what some Christians believed were the pressing theological and social issues of their day. In their interaction with major religious issues in the Old Testament, they demonstrate what it means to have one foot firmly planted in the tradition. In their insistence on the need for a new covenant, a new sacrifice, a new form of worship, they show how believers need to have the other foot in the future. The author of Hebrews clearly sees the need to interpret old beliefs in the light of current culture. In so doing, he made the gospel more accessible to his original readers as they looked ahead with uncertainty.

 Want to Know More?

About Timothy? See F.F. Bruce, *The Pauline Circle* (Grand Rapids: Wm. B. Eerdmans Publishing Co., 1985), 29–34.

When we read the same book, of course, we see something quite different. Many of the illustrations and theological arguments have lost their significance for us. In such a way, Hebrews helps us understand why there needs to be more than one book in the New Testament. The good news of Jesus Christ is not fully contained in just one Gospel, one letter, or one sermon or tract. Hebrews shows us how important it is for us to develop new metaphors of faith, just as its author did. Although the concept of Jesus as the high priest may no longer be relevant to the lives of Christians today, we need to explore the overall impact of the insight that Jesus is superior to everything and everyone on heaven and earth and rediscover what that truth means to us in the twenty-first century. Perhaps even as we develop new images drawn from quantum physics, biology, or the discoveries we make in the exploration of outer space, we may learn more concretely what it means to believe that Jesus is the same yesterday, today, and tomorrow.

? Questions for Reflection

1. How is good conduct a major criterion for leadership in the church? What do you think a congregation should do if leaders act irresponsibly or unethically?
2. What does it mean to you to say that Jesus is the great shepherd of the sheep? Why do you think that Psalm 23 is still so popular, even though most American Christians never even see sheep?
3. How can God bring you peace of mind in time of trouble? Have you ever had an experience where your faith in Christ brought you comfort even though you were in great turmoil?
4. How do you know that your conscience is good? Is it possible that we can be misled by rationalizations or a bad conscience?

Bibliography

Achtemeier, Paul J., ed. *HarperCollins Bible Dictionary*. San Francisco: HarperCollins, 1985, 1986.

Adkins, Leslie, and Roy A. Adkins. *Handbook to Life in Ancient Rome*. New York and Oxford: Oxford University Press, 1994.

Alexander, Pat, and David Alexander. *Zondervan Handbook to the Bible*. Grand Rapids: Zondervan Publishing House, 1999.

Attridge, Harold W. *The Epistle to the Hebrews*. Hermeneia. Philadelphia: Fortress Press, 1989.

Bond, Helen K. *Caiaphas: Friend of Rome and Judge of Jesus?* Louisville, Ky.: Westminster John Knox Press, 2004.

Bruce, F.F. *The Pauline Circle*. Grand Rapids: Wm. B. Eerdmans Publishing Co., 1985.

Gench, Frances Taylor. *Hebrews and James*. Westminster Bible Companion. Louisville, Ky.: Westminster John Knox Press, 1996.

Guthrie, George. *The Structure of Hebrews, A Text-Linguistic Analysis*. Leiden: E. J. Brill, 1994.

Harrington,Daniel J. *What Are They Saying about the Letter to the Hebrews?* Mahwah, N.J.: Paulist Press, 2005.

Harvey, Van A. *A Handbook of Theological Terms*. New York: Macmillan Company, 1964.

Horsley, G.H.R. *New Documents Illustrating Early Christianity*. Vol. 4. Marrickville, Australia: Southwood Press, 1987.

Jeffers, James S. *The Greco-Roman World of the New Testament Era: Exploring the Background of Early Christianity*. Downers Grove, Ill.: InterVarsity Press, 1999.

Johnson, Earl S., Jr. *Galatians and Ephesians*. Basic Bible Commentary. Nashville: Abingdon Press, 1994.

———. *James, First and Second Peter, First, Second, and Third John, and Jude*. Basic Bible Commentary. Nashville: Abingdon Press, 1994.

Johnson, Luke Timothy. *Hebrews: A Commentary*. New Testament Library. Louisville, Ky.: Westminster John Knox Press, 2006.

Koester, Craig R. *Hebrews: A New Translation*. Anchor Bible. New York: Doubleday, 2001.

Long, Thomas G. *Hebrews: A Bible Commentary for Teaching and Preaching*. Louisville, Ky.: Westminster John Knox Press, 1997.

Longenecker, Bruce W. *The Art and Theology of the New Testament Chain-Link Transitions.* Waco, Tex.: Baylor University Press, 2005.

Nelson, Richard D. *Joshua.* Old Testament Library. Louisville, Ky.: Westminster John Knox Press, 1997.

Sakenfeld, Katherine Doob, ed. *The New Interpreter's Dictionary of the Bible: A–C,* Vol. 1. Nashville: Abingdon Press, 2006.

Westfall, Cynthia Long. *A Discourse Analysis of the Letter to the Hebrews: The Relationship between Form and Meaning.* London: T. & T. Clark, 2005.

Wolcott, Leonard T. *Hebrews.* Basic Bible Commentary, Vol. 27. Nashville: Abingdon Press, 1988.

Interpretation Bible Studies
Leader's Guide

Interpretation Bible Studies (IBS), for adults and older youth, are flexible, attractive, easy-to-use, and filled with solid information about the Bible. IBS helps Christians discover the guidance and power of the scriptures for living today. Perhaps you are leading a church school class, a mid-week Bible study group, or a youth group meeting, or simply using this in your own personal study. Whatever the setting may be, we hope you find this *Leader's Guide* helpful. Since every context and group is different, this *Leader's Guide* does not presume to tell you how to structure Bible study for your situation. Instead, the *Leader's Guide* seeks to offer choices—a number of helpful suggestions for leading a successful Bible study using IBS.

> "The church that no longer hears the essential message of the Scriptures soon ceases to understand what it is for and is open to be captured by the dominant religious philosophy of the moment." —James D. Smart, *The Strange Silence of the Bible in the Church: A Study in Hermeneutics* (Philadelphia: Westminster Press, 1970), 10.

How Should I Teach IBS?

1. Explore the Format

There is a wealth of information in IBS, perhaps more than you can use in one session. In this case, more is better. IBS has been designed to give you a well-stocked buffet of content and teachable insights. Pick and choose what suits your group's needs. Perhaps you will want to split units into two or more sessions, or combine units into a single session. Perhaps you will decide to use only a portion of a unit and then move on to the next unit. *There is not a structured theme or teaching focus to each unit that must be followed for IBS to be used.* Rather, IBS offers the flexibility to adjust to whatever suits your context.

"The more we bring to the Bible, the more we get from the Bible."—William Barclay, *A Beginner's Guide to the New Testament* (Louisville, Ky.: Westminster John Knox Press, 1995), vii.

A recent survey of both professional and volunteer church educators revealed that their number-one concern was that Bible study materials be teacher-friendly. IBS is indeed teacher-friendly in two important ways. First, since IBS provides abundant content and a flexible design, teachers can shape the lessons creatively, responding to the needs of the group and employing a wide variety of teaching methods. Second, those who wish more specific suggestions for planning the sessions can find them at the Westminster John Knox Press Web site (**www.wjkbooks.com**). Here, you can access a study guide with teaching suggestions for each IBS unit as well as helpful quotations, selections from Bible dictionaries and encyclopedias, and other teaching helps.

IBS is not only teacher-friendly but also discussion-friendly. Given the opportunity, most adults and young people relish the chance to talk about the kind of issues raised in IBS. The secret, then, is to determine what works with your group, what will get them to talk. Several good methods for stimulating discussion are presented in this *Leader's Guide,* and once you learn your group, you can apply one of these methods and get the group discussing the Bible and its relevance in their lives.

The format of every IBS unit consists of several features:

a. Body of the Unit. This is the main content, consisting of interesting and informative commentary on the passage and scholarly insight into the biblical text and its significance for Christians today.

b. Sidebars. These are boxes that appear scattered throughout the body of the unit, with maps, photos, quotations, and intriguing ideas. Some sidebars can be identified quickly by a symbol, or icon, that helps the reader know what type of information can be found in that sidebar. There are icons for illustrations, key terms, pertinent quotes, and more.

c. Want to Know More? Each unit includes a "Want to Know More?" section that guides learners who wish to dig deeper and consult other resources. If your church library does not have the resources mentioned, you can look up the information in other standard Bible dictionaries, encyclopedias, and handbooks, or you can find much of this information at the Westminster John Knox Press Web site (see last page of this Guide).

d. Questions for Reflection. The unit ends with questions to help the learners think more deeply about the biblical passage and its pertinence for today. These questions are provided as examples only, and teachers are encouraged both to develop their own list of questions and to gather questions from the group. These discussion questions do not usually have specific "correct" answers. Again, the flexibility of IBS allows you to use these questions at the end of the group time, at the beginning, interspersed throughout, or not at all.

> "The trick is to make the Bible our book." — Duncan S. Ferguson, *Bible Basics: Mastering the Content of the Bible* (Louisville, Ky.: Westminster John Knox Press, 1995), 3.

2. Select a Teaching Method

Here are ten suggestions. The format of IBS allows you to choose what direction you will take as you plan to teach. Only you will know how your lesson should best be designed for your group. Some adult groups prefer the lecture method, while others prefer a high level of free-ranging discussion. Many youth groups like interaction, activity, the use of music, and the chance to talk about their own experiences and feelings. Here is a list of a few possible approaches. Let your own creativity add to the list!

a. Let's Talk about What We've Learned. In this approach, all group members are requested to read the scripture passage and the IBS unit before the group meets. Ask the group members to make notes about the main issues, concerns, and questions they see in the passage. When the group meets, these notes are collected, shared, and discussed. This method depends, of course, on the group's willingness to do some "homework."

b. What Do We Want and Need to Know? This approach begins by having the whole group read the scripture passage together. Then, drawing from your study of the IBS, you, as the teacher, write on a board or flip chart two lists:

(1) Things we should know to better understand this passage (content information related to the passage, for example, historical insights about political contexts, geographical landmarks, economic nuances, etc.), and

> "Although small groups can meet for many purposes and draw upon many different resources, the one resource which has shaped the life of the Church more than any other throughout its long history has been the Bible."—Roberta Hestenes, *Using the Bible in Groups* (Philadelphia: Westminster Press, 1983), 14.

(2) Four or five "important issues we should talk about regarding this passage" (with implications for today—how the issues in the biblical context continue into today, for example, issues of idolatry or fear).

Allow the group to add to either list, if they wish, and use the lists to lead into a time of learning, reflection, and discussion. This approach is suitable for those settings where there is little or no advanced preparation by the students.

c. Hunting and Gathering. Start the unit by having the group read the scripture passage together. Then divide the group into smaller clusters (perhaps having as few as one person), each with a different assignment. Some clusters can discuss one or more of the "Questions for Reflection." Others can look up key terms or people in a Bible dictionary or track down other biblical references found in the body of the unit. After the small clusters have had time to complete their tasks, gather the entire group again and lead them through the study material, allowing each cluster to contribute what it learned.

d. From Question Mark to Exclamation Point. This approach begins with contemporary questions and then moves to the biblical content as a response to those questions. One way to do this is for you to ask the group, at the beginning of the class, a rephrased version of one or more of the "Questions for Reflection" at the end of the study unit. For example, one of the questions at the end of the unit on Exodus 3:1–4:17 in the IBS *Exodus* volume reads,

> Moses raised four protests, or objections, to God's call. Contemporary people also raise objections to God's call. In what ways are these similar to Moses' protests? In what ways are they different?

This question assumes familiarity with the biblical passage about Moses, so the question would not work well before the group has explored the passage. However, try rephrasing this question as an opening exercise; for example:

Here is a thought experiment: Let's assume that God, who called people in the Bible to do daring and risky things, still calls people today to tasks of faith and courage. In the Bible, God called Moses from a burning bush and called Isaiah in a moment of ecstatic worship in the Temple. How do you think God's call is experienced by people today? Where do you see evidence of people saying "yes" to God's call? When people say "no" or raise an objection to God's call, what reasons do they give (to themselves, to God)?

Posing this or a similar question at the beginning will generate discussion and raise important issues, and then it can lead the group into an exploration of the biblical passage as a resource for thinking even more deeply about these questions.

e. Let's Go to the Library. From your church library, your pastor's library, or other sources, gather several good commentaries on the book of the Bible you are studying. Among the trustworthy commentaries are those in the Interpretation series (John Knox Press) and the Westminster Bible Companion series (Westminster John Knox Press). Divide your groups into smaller clusters and give one commentary to each cluster (one or more of the clusters can be given the IBS volume instead of a full-length commentary). Ask each cluster to read the biblical passage you are studying and then to read the section of the commentary that covers that passage (if your group is large, you may want to make photocopies of the commentary material with proper permission, of course). The task of each cluster is to name the two or three most important insights they discover about the biblical passage by reading and talking together about the commentary material. When you reassemble the larger group to share these insights, your group will gain not only a variety of insights about the passage but also a sense that differing views of the same text are par for the course in biblical interpretation.

f. Working Creatively Together. Begin with a creative group task, tied to the main thrust of the study. For example, if the study is on the Ten Commandments, a parable, or a psalm, have the group rewrite the Ten Commandments, the parable, or the psalm in contemporary language. If the passage is an epistle, have the group write a letter to their own congregation. Or if the study is a narrative, have the group role-play the characters in the story or write a page describing the story from the point of view of one of the characters. After completion of the task, read and discuss the biblical passage, asking for interpretations and applications from the group and tying in IBS material as it fits the flow of the discussion.

g. Singing Our Faith. Begin the session by singing (or reading) together a hymn that alludes to the biblical passage being studied (or to the theological themes in the passage). For example, if you are studying the unit from the IBS volume on Psalm 121, you can sing "I to the Hills Will Lift My Eyes," "Sing Praise to God, Who Reigns Above," or another hymn based on Psalm 121. Let the group reflect on the thoughts and feelings evoked by the hymn, then move to the biblical passage, allowing the biblical text and the IBS material to underscore, clarify, refine, and deepen the discussion stimulated by the hymn. If you are ambitious, you may ask the group to write a new hymn at the end of the study! (Many hymnals have indexes in the back or companion volumes that help the user match hymns to scripture passages or topics.)

h. Fill in the Blanks. In order to help the learners focus on the content of the biblical passage, at the beginning of the session ask each member of the group to read the biblical passage and fill out a brief questionnaire about the details of the passage (provide a copy for each learner or write the questions on the board). For example, if you are studying the unit in the IBS *Matthew* volume on Matthew 22:1–14, the questionnaire could include questions such as the following:

— In this story, Jesus compares the kingdom of heaven to what?
— List the various responses of those who were invited to the king's banquet but who did not come.
— When his invitation was rejected, how did the king feel? What did the king do?
— In the second part of the story, when the king saw a man at the banquet without a wedding garment, what did the king say? What did the man say? What did the king do?
— What is the saying found at the end of this story?

Gather the group's responses to the questions and perhaps encourage discussion. Then lead the group through the IBS material, helping the learners to understand the meanings of these details and the significance of the passage for today. Feeling creative? Instead of a fill-in-the-blanks questionnaire, create a crossword puzzle from names and words in the biblical passage.

i. Get the Picture. In this approach, stimulate group discussion by incorporating a painting, photograph, or other visual object into the lesson. You can begin by having the group examine and comment on this visual, or you can introduce the visual later in the lesson—it depends on the object used. If, for example, you are studying the unit Exodus 3:1–4:17 in the IBS *Exodus* volume, you may want to view Paul Koli's very colorful painting *The Burning Bush.* Two sources for this painting are *The Bible through Asian Eyes,* edited by Masao Takenaka and Ron O'Grady (National City, Calif.: Pace Publishing Co., 1991), and *Imaging the Word: An Arts and Lectionary Resource,* vol. 3, edited by Susan A. Blain (Cleveland: United Church Press, 1996).

j. Now Hear This. Especially if your class is large, you may want to use the lecture method. As the teacher, you prepare a presentation on the biblical passage, using as many resources as you have available plus your own experience, but following the content of the IBS unit as a guide. You can make the lecture even more lively by asking the learners at various points along the way to refer to the visuals and quotes found in the "sidebars." A place can be made for questions (like the ones at the end of the unit)—either at the close of the lecture or at strategic points along the way.

> "It is . . . important to call a Bible study group back to what the text being discussed actually says, especially when an individual has gotten off on some tangent." —Richard Robert Osmer, *Teaching for Faith: A Guide for Teachers of Adult Classes* (Louisville, Ky.: Westminster/John Knox Press, 1992), 71.

3. Keep These Teaching Tips in Mind

There are no surefire guarantees for a teaching success. However, the following suggestions can increase the chances for a successful study:

a. Always Know Where the Group Is Headed. Take ample time beforehand to prepare the material. Know the main points of the study, and know the destination. Be flexible, and encourage discussion, but don't lose sight of where you are headed.

b. Ask Good Questions; Don't Be Afraid of Silence. Ideally, a discussion blossoms spontaneously from the reading of the scripture. But more often than not, a discussion must be drawn from the group members by a series of well-chosen questions. After asking each question, give the group members time to answer. Let them think, and don't be threatened by a season of silence. Don't feel that every question must have an answer and that as leader, you must supply every answer. Facilitate discussion by getting the group members to cooperate with each other. Sometimes the original question can be restated. Sometimes it is helpful to ask a follow-up question like "What makes this a hard question to answer?"

Ask questions that encourage explanatory answers. Try to avoid questions that can be answered simply "Yes" or "No." Rather than asking, "Do you think Moses was frightened by the burning bush?" ask, "What do you think Moses was feeling and experiencing as he stood before the burning bush?" If group members answer with just one word, ask a follow-up question like "Why do you think this is so?" Ask questions about their feelings and opinions, mixed within questions about facts or details. Repeat their responses or restate their response to reinforce their contributions to the group.

> "Studies of learning reveal that while people remember approximately 10% of what they hear, they remember up to 90% of what they say. Therefore, to increase the amount of learning that occurs, increase the amount of talking about the Bible which each member does." —Roberta Hestenes, *Using the Bible in Groups* (Philadelphia: Westminster Press, 1983), 17.

Most studies can generate discussion by asking open-ended questions. Depending on the group, several types of questions can work. Some groups will respond well to content questions that can be answered from reading the IBS comments or the biblical passage. Others will respond well to questions about feelings or thoughts. Still others will respond to questions that challenge them to new thoughts or that may not have exact answers. Be sensitive to the group's dynamic in choosing questions.

Some suggested questions are: What is the point of the passage? Who are the main characters? Where is the tension in the story? Why does it say (this) _____, and not (that) _____? What raises questions for you? What terms need defining? What are the new ideas? What doesn't make sense? What bothers or troubles you about this passage? What keeps you from living the truth of this passage?

c. Don't Settle for the Ordinary. There is nothing like a surprise. Think of special or unique ways to present the ideas of the study. Upset the applecart of the ordinary. Even though the passage may be familiar, look for ways to introduce suspense. Remember that a little mystery can capture the imagination. Change your routine.

Along with the element of surprise, humor can open up a discussion. Don't be afraid to laugh. A well-chosen joke or cartoon may present the central theme in a way that a lecture would have stymied.

Sometimes a passage is too familiar. No one speaks up because everyone feels that all that could be said has been said. Choose an unfamiliar translation from which to read, or if the passage is from a Gospel, compare the story across two or more Gospels and note differences. It is amazing what insights can be drawn from seeing something strange in what was thought to be familiar.

d. Feel Free to Supplement the IBS Resources with Other Material. Consult other commentaries or resources. Tie in current events with the lesson. Scour newspapers or magazines for stories that touch on the issues of the study. Sometimes the lyrics of a song, or a section of prose from a well-written novel, will be just the right seasoning for the study.

e. And Don't Forget to Check the Web. You can download a free study guide from our Web site (**www.wjkbooks.com**). Each study guide includes several possibilities for applying the teaching methods suggested above for individual IBS units.

f. Stay Close to the Biblical Text. Don't forget that the goal is to learn the Bible. Return to the text again and again. Avoid making the mistake of reading the passage only at the beginning of the study, and then wandering away to comments on top of comments from that point on. Trust in the power

> "The Bible is literature, but it is much more than literature. It is the holy book of Jews and Christians, who find there a manifestation of God's presence." —Kathleen Norris, *The Psalms* (New York: Riverhead Books, 1997), xxii.

and presence of the Holy Spirit to use the truths of the passage to work within the lives of the study participants.

What If I Am Using IBS in Personal Bible Study?

If you are using IBS in your personal Bible study, you can experiment and explore a variety of ways. You may choose to read straight through the study without giving any attention to the sidebars or other features. Or you may find yourself interested in a question or unfamiliar with a key term, and you can allow the sidebars "Want to

Know More?" and "Questions for Reflection" to lead you into deeper learning on these issues. Perhaps you will want to have a few commentaries or a Bible dictionary available to pursue what interests you. As was suggested in one of the teaching methods above, you may want to begin with the questions at the end, and then read the Bible passage followed by the IBS material. Trust the IBS resources to provide good and helpful information, and then follow your interests!

 Want to Know More?

About leading Bible study groups? See Roberta Hestenes, *Using the Bible in Groups* (Philadelphia: Westminster Press, 1983).

About basic Bible content? See Duncan S. Ferguson, *Bible Basics: Mastering the Content of the Bible* (Louisville, Ky.: Westminster John Knox Press, 1995); William M. Ramsay, *The Westminster Guide to the Books of the Bible* (Louisville, Ky.: Westminster John Knox Press, 1994).

About the development of the Bible? See John Barton, *How the Bible Came to Be* (Louisville, Ky.: Westminster John Knox Press, 1997).

About the meaning of difficult terms? See Donald K. McKim, *Westminster Dictionary of Theological Terms* (Louisville, Ky.: Westminster John Knox Press, 1996); Paul J. Achtemeier, *Harper's Bible Dictionary* (San Francisco: Harper & Row, 1985).

To download a free IBS study guide,

visit our Web site at

www.wjkbooks.com